C. S. Lewis

Chronicler of Narnia

Mary Dodson Wade

Enslow Publishers, Inc.

40 Industrial Road	PO Box 38
Box 398	Aldershot
Berkeley Heights, NJ 07922	Hants GU12 6BP
USA	UK

http://www.enslow.com

Dedication

For Dana, who knew him first,
and for Jeanne, who saw what I did not

Library of Congress Cataloging-in-Publication Data

Wade, Mary Dodson.
    C.S. Lewis : chronicler of Narnia / by Mary Dodson Wade.
       p. cm.— (Authors teens love)
    Includes bibliographical references and index.
    ISBN-10: 0-7660-2446-6
    1. Lewis, C. S. (Clive Staples), 1898–1963—Juvenile literature.
    2. Authors, English—20th century—Biography—Juvenile literature.
    3. Fantasy fiction—Authorship—Juvenile literature. 4. Narnia (Imaginary place)—Juvenile literature. I. Title. II. Series.
    PR6023.E926Z937 2005
    823'.912—dc22

                            2005014963

    ISBN-13: 978-0-7660-2446-5

Printed in the United States of America

10 9 8 7 6 5 4 3 2

Illustration Credits: Used by permission of The Marion E. Wade Center, Wheaton College, Wheaton, IL, except pp. 45 and 77, photos taken by Mary Dodson Wade, Courtesy of the Marion E. Wade Center.

Cover Illustration: Used by permission of The Marion E. Wade Center, Wheaton College, Wheaton, IL (foreground); JupiterImages Corporation/ Corel Corporation (background).

Contents

CHAPTER 1

The Little End Room

"There was a boy called Eustace Clarence Scrubb, and he almost deserved it."[1]

So begins with *The Voyage of the Dawn Treader,* one of the books published in *The Chronicles of Narnia.* C. S. Lewis, literary scholar, had no children of his own, but he understood how they felt. This line, perhaps the funniest in all the series, comes from a man who renamed himself.

Albert and Flora Lewis got an early glimpse of the independent thinking of their younger son. Clive Staples Lewis was less than four years old when he stood before his parents, pointed to himself, and announced, "He is Jacksie."[2] After several days of refusing to answer to his real name, C. S. Lewis, for the rest of his life, was simply "Jack" to his family and friends.

Lewis was born in an inner suburb of Belfast,

Ireland, on November 29, 1898. His arrival caused the usual resentment in his brother Warren, born three years earlier. This rivalry disappeared shortly, and the brothers became the closest of friends.[3]

Albert Lewis was a respected police court solicitor (lawyer). He was witty, with a quick mind, a short temper, and a sense of honor. Although not large, he had a commanding presence and voice. His well-run office provided a good living for the family.[4]

Albert was the first of his family to hold a professional job. His grandfather had been a farmer in Wales. His father immigrated to Northern Ireland and worked with an iron shipbuilding firm. Albert studied at Lurgan College, where he became a favorite pupil of headmaster William T. Kirkpatrick. Financial problems forced his withdrawal.[5] He had a gift of oratory, and if the family had been wealthy, he probably would have entered politics. As it was, he opened a law office and was rarely far from it for the rest of his life.

Flora Hamilton Lewis came from a family of clergymen, lawyers, and sailors. Her mother was an eccentric woman who lived in a tumbled-down house full of cats. This outspoken woman openly supported the right of the Irish people to govern themselves during the time when all of Ireland was part of Great Britain. It was not a popular view in this family with British roots.[6]

Flora had studied at Queen's College in Belfast. At age eighteen, she earned a degree and took highest honors in geometry and algebra. Five years later she earned honors in logic and mathematics.[7] Unfortunately, her mathematical ability escaped her sons.

Albert patiently waited eight years for her to accept his proposal. Their wedding took place on August 19, 1894. Albert selected a diamond star bracelet, two

Jack Lewis's childhood was spent in a comfortable middle-class home in Belfast, Ireland.

pendants, and a diamond hoop bracelet as his wife's wedding present. A careful man who always feared that he would end in poverty, he also gave her a set of rules on spending money wisely.[8]

Flora enjoyed her children. From the time the boys were very young, she took them for seaside holidays. Sea baths seemed to help her headaches and asthma. Albert Lewis rarely joined them. When he did, he was always impatient to get back to his office.[9]

The boys loved these holidays. Swimming became a lifelong habit for Lewis, both in the sea and in rivers and lakes. He confided to a child that his favorite thing, even in the bathtub, was to lie submerged like a hippopotamus and open his eyes underwater.[10]

During these vacations, Flora wrote daily to Albert. She reported reading *The Three Bears* to baby Jack. He was learning to talk. Warren had the sniffles. Jack, in a clear voice, told his brother, "Warnie, wipe nose." The following year Flora and Warren were asking riddles. To her amazement, Jack sometimes joined in. Even before Jack could write, he dictated stories to his father on Saturday evenings.[11]

Through the years, both Jack and Warren came to dread conversations with their father. He lectured them with long talks and endless stories they called "wheezes." Any action on their part that angered him launched a firestorm of words and law phrases. When the boys were young, they bonded together against this. They stopped being intimidated when as youngsters they cut up a ladder to make tent poles. Their father's rage erupted into words so high-flown that the boys could barely hide their laughter. Even as an adult, C. S. Lewis found visits with his father a burden. He tried to arrange to be at home when Warren was there. But he did not fail to write weekly.[12]

In spite of Albert Lewis's inability to relate to his children, he loved his family. As his practice grew, he built a new house on the outskirts of Belfast. When Jack was seven years old, they moved into Leeborough, or Little Lea as they called it. Warren left almost immediately for boarding school, but Little Lea remained the brothers' home until their father's death nearly twenty-five years later.

As grown men, they felt their father had been cheated by the builders, but as children they thought it was perfect. The walls didn't line up. There were nooks and passageways to explore.

> **Even before [Lewis] could write, he dictated stories to his father.**

The boys quickly claimed part of the attic they called "the little end room." There they created stories to amuse themselves. Lewis treasured this undisturbed time to exercise his imagination. He later wrote, "I am the product of long corridors, empty sunlit rooms, . . . attics explored in solitude."[13]

The bedroom Warren and Jack shared looked out on the Castlereagh Hills. From the front door of Little Lea, they could see ships in the Belfast harbor. Even distant Scotland was visible on a clear day.[14]

Because of the wet climate, the boys were often kept indoors for fear they would become ill. Lewis suffered colds and sore throats throughout his life. In adulthood, he felt sorry for modern children who had no time to enjoy the solitude he loved. But he envied raincoats and rubber boots that allowed them to go outdoors on rainy days.[15]

Jack and Warren had few friends, but they were not

C. S. Lewis works behind his desk as an adult, after having grown up reading his favorite books as a child while seated at a desk.

lonely. They had each other and their books. Warren's first book was a huge illustrated *Mother Goose*, given to him by his father when he was three. Jack owned copies of Beatrix Potter's *Peter Rabbit* and *Squirrel Nutkin* soon after they were published. His interest spread to knights after reading Arthur Conan Doyle's *Sir Nigel* and Mark Twain's *A Connecticut Yankee in King Arthur's Court*. Later, E. Nesbit's *Five Children and It* opened up the world of time travel. One of his favorite books was a lavishly illustrated version of *Gulliver's Travels* by Jonathan Swift. In his father's study he read stacks of the comical *Punch* magazines.[16]

While writing his own stories, Jack sat at a little desk made especially for him. With pencils and paint he created "Animal-Land." The main character was

Lord Big, a frog dressed in high, stiff collar and the coat and trousers of an English gentleman. A bird named Vicount Puddiphat was a fancy dresser with a top hat and spats on his shoes.[17]

Warren set his stories in "India." The boys' Grandfather Hamilton had visited that country. Warren was fascinated with maps. At age five, he received a globe from his father. While Albert Lewis was in London trying a case in the House of Lords, Warren drew a creditable world map for him.[18] His stories were filled with ships and trains.

Eventually, the boys meshed the two creations into a country they called "Boxen." After Warren left for school, Jack continued the stories. He reported to Warren about revolts and "convulsions." These usually involved King Bunny being kidnaped again.[19]

When he was about thirty, Lewis began an "encyclopedia" for Boxen, but he found it impossible to reconcile products with the climate where they were found. Perhaps, he suggested, Boxen was tilted on a different axis from the earth. He decided he would let some "future Boxenologist" solve this puzzle.[20]

Lewis said a physical deformity made him an author. Both he and Warren could not bend the first joint of their thumbs. They could grasp a pen, but they could not hold a hammer. Jack longed to build castles but he was too clumsy. Instead, he created stories with castles.[21]

Both Albert and Flora Lewis were avid readers. In Little Lea, every room and hallway had overflowing bookcases. Books sat two deep on the stair-landing bookcase. Shoulder-high stacks stood in the attic. On rainy days, C. S. Lewis never had trouble finding a book that he had not read before.[22]

The boys were not forbidden to read anything. This

wide reading expanded Jack's vocabulary to the point that adults talked to him just to hear the words he used. When he realized what they were doing, he spoke very little until he was alone again with Warren.[23]

This unfettered reading may have been the cause of recurring nightmares he suffered. In one, ghosts danced with jerky movements like machines that had come to life. The other had giant insects. One of his nursery books had a lever that made the pincers of a large beetle reach for a tiny child. It wasn't until Jack was in his teens that he discovered a book called *Ants, Bees and Wasps* that cured his nightmares about insects.[24]

Some of the books in the house were suitable, some were not. In middle age he commented, "Those of us who are blamed when old for reading childish books were blamed when children for reading books too old for us."[25]

Doting parents gave him a happy childhood. Nursemaid Lizzie Endicott added Irish folk tales. She was not on the social strata of the Lewis family, but her goodness taught Lewis that social standing had nothing to do with a person's value.[26]

The boys loved nature. When he was very young, Warren filled the lid of a cookie tin with moss and brought it to Jack. The sight of the little garden gave him a sudden, intense moment of pleasure that he recalled for the rest of his life. He got this same stab of pleasure from reading Beatrix Potter's *Squirrel Nutkin*. Later, standing next to a flowering currant bush in the garden, he experienced the feeling again. He called it Joy and longed for it to come again.[27]

In 1908 tragedy struck. Flora Lewis died of cancer on Albert Lewis's forty-fifth birthday. Grief stricken, he recorded her death in his diary. Then he copied the quotation from Shakespeare's *King Lear* that appeared on the calendar that day—"Men must endure their going hence." He put these words on his wife's gravestone. After his death, his sons found the calendar page among his papers.[28]

For Jack, the loss of his mother was a terrible blow. His anchor was gone. Albert Lewis was inconsolable. Always prone to outbursts of anger, he now flew into rages or broke down weeping. His distressed sons did not know where to turn.[29]

Within three weeks of Flora Lewis's death, nine-year-old Jack was on his way to England. Wearing hot itchy clothes, a bowler hat that felt like an iron ring, and boots that hurt his feet, he boarded a boat with Warren to face the horrors of an English boarding school.[30]

Chapter 2

"Are Athletes Better than Scholars?"

The trip across the Irish Sea shortly after his mother's death was the first of many Jack made to attend school in England. Albert Lewis felt his sons were better off there than at home, but, for Jack, the loss he felt for his mother only deepened. By the time he reached Watford, near London, he hated everything. Even the haystacks were not the right shape. But the real horror turned out to be the school itself.[1]

Warren had been at Wynyard House for three years. Albert Lewis was unaware of the deplorable conditions at the once respected school. Reverend Robert Capron, headmaster, flew into rages and beat the students for no apparent cause. There were no organized activities. Discipline was cruel. No learning took place. Warren recalled doing the same arithmetic over and over again. He commented, "It is a significant fact that I cannot remember one single piece of information which was imparted to me at Wynyard."[2]

Barely two weeks into the school term Jack wrote his father demanding to come home immediately. Albert Lewis, unaware and resistant to change, did nothing.[3]

In order to have something to read, a group of boys pooled their magazines. Jack supplied *The Strand*, the magazine where *The Adventures of Sherlock Holmes* first appeared.[4]

Capron's religion emphasized an angry God. The church Lewis attended preached about the awful fate awaiting sinners. Young Jack spent wakeless nights staring at the moon through curtainless windows. He wrote down rules to help him become a better person. During one visit home, his father pulled the rules out of his pocket. Embarrassed, Jack grabbed them and threw them in the fire. This incident became a symbol of his father's prying into his affairs. It triggered a resentment that lasted until his father died.[5]

Albert Lewis did not understand children and did not always do the right things. Jack asked for a microscope the Christmas he was eleven. Then he wrote telling his father not to get it because he would have to kill insects in order to look at them. He got the microscope anyway.[6]

Jack remained at the school after Warren left. He shivered in unheated rooms. Nightmares disturbed his sleep.[7]

His release came in 1910. Capron wrote Albert Lewis that he was closing Wynyard School. Less than two years later, Capron died in an insane asylum. Lewis's memory of his agony at Wynyard led him to call the school Belsen, the name of a World War II Nazi concentration camp. His only happiness came on holidays when he and Warren returned to the "little end room" at Little Lea.[8]

Whenever the boys came home to Belfast, Flora Lewis's cousin, Mary Ewart, provided social life. Her husband, Sir William Quartus Ewart, had been a partner in one of the biggest flax-spinning and linen manufacture businesses in Belfast. Their large house, Glenmachan, was near Little Lea.[9]

The three Ewart daughters were much older, but they showered kindness on the Lewis boys. Hope Ewart, the oldest, took Jack to see *Peter Pan*. They organized parties and picnics. At one party everyone came representing a book title. Teenage Jack showed up with a piece of paper saying "Soldiers Three." Nobody guessed that it was *The Three Musketeers*. Jack

Jack and Warren Lewis were friends as well as brothers. Jack often explored on his bicycle.

hated the dances. The stiff clothing made the large, clumsy boy even more uncomfortable. To him, these activities wasted precious time with Warren.[10]

After Wynyard closed, Jack briefly attended a school run by Campbell College. It was in Belfast about a mile from Little Lea. Plagued with the colds and sore throats, he spent much of his time in the school's infirmary. After three months he came home with such a bad cough that his father did not send him back.

In the short time Jack was at Campbell, English teacher J. A. McNeill introduced him to "Sohrab and Rustum." This epic poem written by Matthew Arnold cast a spell on him from its very first words. Because of it, he was able to enjoy Greek poet Homer's *Iliad*. Many years later when Lewis was asked about his favorite poems, he listed "The Saga of King Olaf" first. "Sohrab and Rustum" was second.[11]

Jack remained home for six weeks. He filled the time with reading, writing, and drawing. For the rest of his life, days of idleness caused by slight illness remained a delight. Years later, he wrote a friend that he had read six books during a "glorious week in bed with the flu."[12]

In January 1911, twelve-year-old Jack enrolled at Cherbourg. This was a preparatory school in Malvern, England, where Warren attended Malvern College. Jack stayed at Cherbourg until July 1913.[13]

On a typical trip to school, he and Warren crossed the Irish Sea and took the train to Liverpool, England. In Liverpool they lounged around the hotel reading magazines and smoking cigarettes before catching the last train to Malvern. On return trips, they sometimes went to performances at the music hall before catching the boat back to Ireland. They tried to hide their smoking from their father. Both brothers continued to smoke for the rest of their lives. To his regret, Lewis was unable to break the habit.[14]

They had no fear of their father's disapproval of the music hall, however. When the boys were home, he often took them to the Belfast Hippodrome on Saturday nights. While Jack's father and brother enjoyed vaudeville, he preferred something more serious. Nevertheless, he treasured these times when his father was in good humor.[15]

At Cherbourg, Norse myths became an obsession with Jack. Longfellow's "The Saga of King Olaf" thrilled him with stories of gods with super powers. He rode through the skies with Valkyries. The strong rhythm of the poetry seemed to lift him into the cold, pale, remote northern sky.[16]

> Norse myths became an obsession with Jack. . . . The strong rhythm of the poetry seemed to lift him into the cold, pale, remote northern sky.

He was fourteen when his first essay appeared in the Cherbourg school magazine. A few months later, the magazine published another Lewis essay entitled, "Are Athletes better than Scholars?"[17]

When time came for entrance examinations to Malvern College, he was running a high fever. The papers were brought to his room, and he did well enough to get a scholarship. His proud father gave him a signed, deluxe edition of an anthology by English author Rudyard Kipling.[18]

By the time Jack entered Malvern in 1913, Warren was no longer there. He had been expelled for smoking. Warren chose an army career. Albert Lewis asked his old schoolmaster, William Kirkpatrick, to prepare Warren for Sandhurst, Britain's military academy. Kirkpatrick had retired and moved to Great Bookham, Surrey, England. He agreed to take Warren and later wrote Albert Lewis, "A nicer boy I never had in the house."[19]

While Warren studied with Kirkpatrick, Jack struggled at Malvern College. Warren was more adaptable than his brother. He had enjoyed the school. For Jack it was agony. His reading was far advanced, and his clumsiness made the intramural games humiliating. He detested the system that allowed older boys to make servants of the younger boys. He made no attempt to fit in and sought escape in the library where he could read in peace.[20]

Warren was convinced that his brother should never have been sent to public school. Both brothers were amused when fifteen years after leaving Malvern College, Lewis was asked to serve on the school's board of directors. He declined the honor.[21]

The bright spot for Jack at Malvern was Latin master Harry Wakelyn Smith. Jack reveled in the way Smith read poetry and acquired the habit of mouthing words silently while reading. Through Smith he developed an appreciation of Latin and Greek poets. In the library he read John Milton and William Butler Yeats. He also found a book of Celtic (Irish) mythology.[22]

Very soon after coming to Malvern, Jack discovered one of Arthur Rackham's illustrations for *Siegfried and the Twilight of the Gods*. This rekindled his love of Norse myths. The feeling intensified when Albert Lewis bought the boys a phonograph. By chance, Jack read a

listing of operas that included German composer
Richard Wagner. Four of the operas are based on *Der
Ring des Niebelungen* (The Ring of the Dwarfs). They
tell the story of Siegfried and his struggle with dwarfs
over a golden ring. Jack was so taken with the operas
that he began his own epic poem called *Loki Bound*.

A little later he heard Wagner's music and was over-
whelmed. He started collecting recordings of Wagner's
music. During a holiday visit to the home of Hope
Ewart, he found a beautifully bound edition of the book
the Siegfried picture appeared in. To Jack, Arthur
Rackham's illustrations made Wagner's music visible.
When Warren learned this, he paid half the cost so that
Jack could buy his own inexpensive copy.[23]

"Pure Northerness" filled Jack's mind. He rode his
bicycle through the countryside looking for places
where Norse stories might have taken place. He longed
for someone to teach him Old Norse language.[24]

While Jack was home for spring holidays in 1914,
he met Arthur Greeves. The Greeves family lived
across the road from Little Lea. Arthur was Warren's
age. He had tried several years earlier to become
friends, but the brothers did not respond. Their time
together was too precious to share. With Warren gone,
fifteen-year-old Jack visited Arthur after learning that
he was ill. He entered Arthur's bedroom and was
startled to see a copy of H. M. A. Guerber's *Myths
of the Norsemen* on the bedside table. "Do *you* like
that?" Jack exclaimed. A surprised Arthur repeated the
question to Jack. Immediately they raced through the
book pointing out favorite passages.[25]

This began a friendship that lasted a lifetime.
Although separated by Jack's schooling, they both
devoured books. One would discover a book and send
a letter flying to the other that he simply *must* buy

this treasure. They described editions in detail. Occasionally, Jack's book buying was interrupted by "a flash of poverty."[26]

Lewis referred to Arthur as his "First Friend"— someone who thought exactly as he did. Arthur played the piano and was a good artist. Arthur taught him to appreciate small, homey things such as a cat sitting by a barn door.[27]

After their first meeting, Jack and Arthur saw each other as often as they could. They corresponded, sometimes weekly, until Lewis's death. Lewis had other friends during his life, but his brother Warren and Arthur Greeves remained closest to him.

Shortly after Lewis found his "First Friend," events elsewhere shattered the world's calm.

Chapter 3

"Never, Never, Never Shall I Have to Play Games Again"

Jack Lewis was an Irish teenager attending school in England when a young rebel in Sarajevo, Bosnia, assassinated Archduke Francis Ferdinand of Austria in June 1914. Nations took sides, and World War I began. Warren Lewis's training at Sandhurst rushed to completion. He finished near the top of his class and by November was in France with the British Expeditionary Forces facing the invasion of German troops.[1]

Jack, facing continued misery at Malvern College, begged his father to let him study with Professor Kirkpatrick. Albert Lewis hesitated; then because Warren had done well with Kirkpatrick, he relented. One thought raced through Jack's mind, "Never, never, never, shall I have to play games again."[2]

In September 1914, Jack made the crossing to

Liverpool and took the train through London down to Great Bookham in Surrey. Happiness seemed to radiate from the valleys and trees. He stepped off the train that Saturday afternoon and met the man who set the pattern for his thinking for the rest of his life. The Lewis brothers nicknamed Kirkpatrick "the Great Knock."[3]

When the professor first saw Jack, he was struck by the resemblance between father and son. He wrote Albert, "It was as if I were looking at yourself." He also noted that Clive, as he always called him, was pleasant and cheerful, with the liveliness of his father.[4]

Jack's first impression of the elderly teacher was that he was looking at Father Time. The tall, thin, muscular gentleman with moustache and bushy side whiskers startled him by grabbing his hand in a vice-like handshake. This was far from the sentimental gentleman his father had described.[5]

As they started toward the Gastons, Kirkpatrick's home, Jack began one of his safe adult conversations. He remarked that the scenery at Great Bookham was "wilder" than he had expected. "Stop!" cried the professor. That word would ring in his ears many times during his stay in Great Bookham. Kirkpatrick demanded to know what the boy meant by "wild" and on what basis he made that statement. Fumbled answers brought additional piercing questions.

Before reaching the house, the teenager had learned his first lesson. Any statement he made would be challenged both for its language and for its content. Challenges came in different levels. "Stop!" indicated that the professor considered the statement useless. A quieter "Excuse" ("Excuse me") meant that the statement needed to be modified. Occasionally there would be an "I hear you." In that case, Kirkpatrick allowed the statement, but Jack still had to defend it.[6]

The habit of making clear statements based on fact became a part of Lewis. For the rest of his life, he demanded the same rigorous examination of facts. When he heard some casual remark, he would boom out, "I challenge that!" With children, he used gentle humor. He responded to one letter by asking whether the children had really put their little sister on the stove to cook.[7]

Kirkpatrick was a no-nonsense teacher. Although Jack had an enormous range of reading, his knowledge of Latin and Greek grammar was weak. The afternoon that they reached the Gastons, Kirkpatrick announced that they would start Greek on Monday. Jack protested that he did not know classical Greek. The professor would change that.

As promised, Kirkpatrick came to Jack's room on Monday after breakfast. The two sat side-by-side on the couch. The professor opened Book I of Homer's *Iliad* and read 100 lines. Then he handed Jack the book and a dictionary and told him to translate what had been read. Jack sat at his table and struggled. He made little progress that first day. Each day the routine was repeated. Each day Jack translated a few more lines than the previous day. Finally he could finish the assigned work. Then it became a game with himself to see how far beyond the assignment he could go. He became so immersed in Greek that he began to think in that language.[8]

Using this same method, teacher and pupil read Virgil, Euripides, and Sophocles in their original languages. With a knowledge of Latin, Jack easily mastered Italian. He even gained a serviceable knowledge of German. Mrs. Kirkpatrick taught him French by reading French novels with him in the evening. She played the piano for him and took him to the ballet.[9]

Life at the Gastons fell into a pattern. A normal day began with breakfast at eight. After the session with Kirkpatrick, Jack was at his desk by nine. Lunch came at one o'clock, followed by an afternoon walk, then tea at 4:30. Supper was at seven. When not working at his studies, Jack read and wrote letters. Bedtime was eleven.[10]

Solitary afternoon nature walks provided time "to shut your mouth, open your eyes and ears." Lewis later credited the fact that his father did not own a car for his great love of walking, but he had developed this habit much earlier.[11]

Letters arrived weekly from his father and from Arthur. The boys wrote incessantly about Norse mythology. Warren's less-frequent letters sometimes contained money for his little brother. Jack spent it on books. When the parcels arrived, he reveled in the feel and smell of the books. He cringed when Kirkpatrick picked them up with dirt-stained hands after working in the garden.[12]

Jack continued to read widely. Kirkpatrick wrote Albert Lewis about his son's "originality of literary judgment." In an egotistical teenage moment, Jack told Arthur that if only those who deserved books were able to get them, the two of them would be the sole support for booksellers.[13]

> Solitary afternoon nature walks provided time "to shut your mouth, open your eyes and ears."

Jack was fond of Rider Haggard's adventure stories. Arthur introduced him to books by Sir Walter Scott, Jane Austen, and the Brontë sisters.

He read H. G. Wells and George Bernard Shaw. Historian Edward Gibbon and French author Voltaire did not excite him. On the last page of Lord Byron's *Don Juan* he wrote, "Never again." The ones he liked, however, he read over and over. "A book's no good to me until I've read it two or three times."[14]

One March day in 1916, Jack walked to Leatherhead. It was a great place to swim in the summer. Because of the distance, he usually took the train back. While browsing the bookstall at the station, he picked up a copy of George MacDonald's *Phantastes: a Faerie Romance*. This story of a young man's dream-like adventures on a life quest overwhelmed him. He fired off a letter to Arthur saying that he simply *must* get a copy and read it.[15]

Reading *Phantastes* changed Lewis's life, but he did not realize why until later. Shortly after coming to the Gastons, he had been confirmed in St. Mark's, the Lewis family church in Belfast. He did this because it was expected of him. Much earlier, he had lost all belief in the existence of God. Studying with Kirkpatrick deepened his antagonism against religion. Kirkpatrick had studied to be a Presbyterian minister but had turned into an atheist. Near the end of their time together, Jack wrote Arthur that he could accept no religion. "There is absolutely no proof for any of them."[16]

The book at the train station changed that. It had a "light," a feeling of good that remained with him long after he finished reading it. He later remarked, "I had not the faintest notion what I had let myself in for by buying *Phantastes*." It was his first step in returning to Christianity.[17]

Jack studied with Kirkpatrick from shortly before his sixteenth birthday and until after his eighteenth. The professor noted Jack's resonant voice and his ability to express himself clearly. Jack had inherited the voice from his father, but the ability to speak effectively came from the professor. Kirkpatrick wrote Albert Lewis, "You may make a writer or a scholar of him, but you'll not make anything else."[18]

Oxford University was the place for such a student. In December 1916, Jack made the trip there to take entrance examinations. The day was bitterly cold. Snow had settled on the turrets of the building, giving it the appearance of a wedding cake. Inside, applicants stayed bundled in overcoats and mufflers and kept their gloves on while writing.[19]

Many students vied for the few openings available. Jack left the examinations and headed home to Ireland feeling that he had failed. He need not have worried. While in Belfast during the Christmas holidays, he got word that he had been accepted at University College at Oxford. That acceptance came, however, with the provision that he pass Responsions, a mathematics examination. Since he was not to report to Oxford until the summer term, he returned to Kirkpatrick for a crash course in mathematics.[20] Kirkpatrick wrote no glowing letters about this session.

CHAPTER 4

"Death in Battle"

By the time Lewis signed into University College in April 1917, one building had been turned into a hospital for wounded soldiers. Sheets shrouded vacant rooms of students who had gone to war.[1]

University, oldest of the Oxford colleges, had been founded in the thirteenth century. Lewis loved the spires and old buildings in the ancient town. Except for a term of army service, he was never again far from Oxford.

He purchased the gown Oxford scholars (students) wore. The dreaded Responsions were scheduled. Then he enrolled in the Officers' Training Corps. He informed his father that the army uniform had cost twice as much as his academic gown.[2]

Within weeks, eighteen-year-old Lewis was called into the army. He trained at Keble, another Oxford college. Marching drills were monotonous, but he joked about losing weight from exercise. His roommate was Edward Courtnay Francis "Paddy" Moore.[3]

Paddy's mother, Janie Moore, was forty-five years old and separated from her husband. Paddy's fourteen-year-old sister Maureen lived with her. In August, Jack had a month's leave but spent the first three weeks with Paddy's family. Janie Moore wrote to Albert Lewis about his charming, likeable son. That did nothing to curb Albert Lewis's resentment that his son had not come home.[4]

While the two soldiers were at the Moore home, Maureen overheard them promise to take care of the other's parent in case one of them did not return from the war.[5] A few weeks later Jack was commissioned as a Second Lieutenant in the Somerset Light Infantry. Paddy was assigned to another unit.

Before being shipped to France, Jack received a 48-hour pass. Instead of trying to get to Ireland, he went again to the Moore's house. He sent a telegram to his father asking him to come. Albert Lewis, unable to understand the message, responded for Jack to send a letter. There was no time. On his nineteenth birthday, C. S. Lewis arrived at the front lines in France without having said goodbye to his father.[6]

Conditions at the front were bad. Water stood knee-deep in the trenches. In spite of this, Lewis did not find the army as bad as he had expected. Officers were polite and considerate. During lulls, he went to underground sleeping quarters and read. He asked his father to send books. He even wrote poetry.[7]

When "trench fever" sent him to a field hospital, he read G. K. Chesterton. To his amazement, he liked this writer in spite of Chesterton's religious views.[8]

Lewis recovered and returned to duty. He never did know why sixty German soldiers suddenly walked out with their hands up and surrendered to him. Then, in April 1918 a shell fired by a British gun behind him exploded nearby. Lewis's companion was killed. Shrapnel entered Lewis's chest, hand, and leg. When Warren heard this, he borrowed a motorcycle and raced fifty miles to see his brother. Fortunately, the wounds were not serious, but Lewis was sent back to England to recover.[9]

He wrote his father regularly. By May 1918, he was able to lie on his right side but not the left. The piece of metal in his chest remained there until it was finally removed in 1944.[10]

A month after he returned to England, Lewis made a short visit to the Kirkpatricks. Kirkpatrick denounced the army's ignorance that shell trajectory changes when weapons become hot from firing. Lewis was amused to learn that he still had "insufficient knowledge of a subject."[11]

During recuperation in a London hospital, Lewis wrote a long letter to his father apologizing for causing the strain in their relationship. He was homesick and begged his father to come. For some reason Albert Lewis did not. Three months went by. Lewis tried to make a joke of it—fellow patients were suggesting that his Irish father was a myth.[12]

This failure on his father's part hurt deeply, but Janie Moore was there. She and Maureen moved to a place near his hospital. Paddy had been officially declared dead. Mrs. Moore wrote Albert Lewis that her hopes had been buried with her son. She wanted to take care of Jack because he had been good to her.[13]

The war left a deep imprint on C. S. Lewis. He never forgot the sight of smashed bodies lying on the battlefield, landscapes made bleak by heavy bombardment. He was haunted by thoughts of the goodness of a slain fellow soldier—a goodness he wanted for his own life.[14]

On November 11, 1918, the armistice ended World War I. Lewis arrived home in Belfast for the Christmas holidays. Warren was there too. Their father served champagne to celebrate.[15]

While Lewis was recovering from his wounds, publisher William Heinemann agreed to print his poems. One of them, "Death in Battle," appeared in the February 1919 issue of *Reveille*. It was included in an anthology to benefit disabled soldiers and sailors. Lewis felt that this would help advertise his forth coming book.[16]

The book, *Spirits in Bondage: A Cycle of Lyrics*, appeared the following month. The author was listed as Clive Hamilton, a combination of his own and his mother's names. Albert Lewis suggested a change in the original title of his son's first book because it was the same as another recently published book.[17]

The poems, called "commonplace" in a review in the *Times Literary Supplement*, were in the traditional style. Lewis intensely disliked modern verse. He hired a clipping service to find other reviews. The one that came was for a logic book published by a California professor also named C. S. Lewis. Nevertheless, the publication of *Spirits in Bondage* at age twenty fueled Lewis's idea that he would be a poet.[18]

CHAPTER 5

"I Love Every Stone of It"

In January 1919, Lewis once again donned his academic gown. He was supremely happy to return to Oxford, the town he described as the most beautiful place he had ever seen. "I love every stone of it."[1]

To his great relief, war veterans were exempted from Responsions. Lewis was convinced that he would never have remained at Oxford if he had been required to pass that examination.[2]

Learning centered on meetings with a tutor. Scholars researched topics assigned by the tutor, prepared an essay, and then came once a week to the tutor's apartment to read and discuss the paper.[3]

On a typical day, Lewis rose at 7:30 A.M. In good weather he went to the river, swam to a bend, and returned on his back, looking up at willow trees. After having breakfast in his room, he read in the library, attended lectures until 1:00 P.M., then rode his bicycle to Mrs. Moore's house for lunch. Afterwards, he worked until tea time and again until dinner. He returned to college about 11:00 P.M. and read for another hour.[4]

The Moores had moved close to Oxford, and Lewis fulfilled his promise to his dead comrade. Money to run the household came from the allowance his father sent. They were often very poor. Lewis's steady stream of letters to his father did not mention his living arrangements, but both Albert and Warren Lewis knew. They felt Mrs. Moore was taking advantage of him.[5]

Lewis's delight was the treasure-trove in Oxford's world-famous Bodleian Library. He found books whose pages were so worm-eaten they were almost impossible to read. Study was challenging, but he reported to his father that he was keeping his "head above the water."[6]

One of his activities was a literary club called the Martlets. This group met and presented papers on different authors. Some very early meetings had been raucous. In 1894 members had shot fireworks and burned effigies of authors they did not like. Minutes of the Martlet meetings were deposited in the Bodleian Library. After Lewis was elected secretary, he joked, "If I am forgotten of all else, at least a specimen of my handwriting will be preserved to posterity."[7]

Lewis did well in his studies. Because of Kirkpatrick's training, he could have skipped the study of Greek and Latin literature called Honor Moderations (Mods). He was advised, however, that if he wanted to become a university professor, he should take these courses. He had no trouble in achieving the highest grade, a First, in Honor Moderations in 1920. To celebrate, he took a walking vacation and read Sir Walter Scott's *Waverley* "to clean out my mind."[8] Week-long walking jaunts with his friends became a pattern for much of his life.

The following term, Lewis began the study of ancient history and philosophy called Greats. During this period he prepared an essay entitled "Optimism." It won the Chancellor's Prize, which he read at the June 1921 graduation ceremony. He wrote Warren about stumbling on his way to the stage.[9]

Sadly, William Kirkpatrick did not live to know about the prize. Three months earlier, Albert Lewis had telegraphed his son with news of Kirkpatrick's death. Lewis responded, "I owe him in the intellectual sphere as much as one human being can owe another." The following year Kirkpatrick's "unrelenting clearness and rigid honesty of thought" carried him to a First in Greats.[10]

With these high marks Lewis hoped to win a philosophy post at Oxford. None was open. He turned down a position at Reading University because the pay was small. It would have also involved an expensive daily train ride since the Moores did not want to move.[11]

University College offered to extend his scholarship for an additional year of study. He reluctantly asked his father for another year of support. Albert Lewis did not hesitate.[12]

Lewis studied English, a course covering Fifteenth to Eighteenth Century authors such as Geoffrey Chaucer, Edmund Spenser, William Shakespeare, and John Milton. He began a study of Old English so that he could read original texts. It surprised no one in 1923 when he took a First in English.[13]

In spite of this extra year of work, no position was open at Oxford. A discouraged Lewis considered going into Civil Service, a job that would need none of his university training. Fortunately, his philosophy tutor, E. F. Carritt, recommended that Lewis take over Carritt's tutorials and lectures in philosophy while the professor was on leave of absence in the United States.[14]

Albert Lewis (left), a successful lawyer, was proud of the academic accomplishments of his son, Jack (right).

The job did not pay much, but Lewis buried himself in the books that he would be discussing with students. He prepared fourteen lectures and joked about delivering them without notes so the audience would not go to sleep.[15]

The following year a fellowship in English Language and Literature became available. Lewis survived stiff competition and was elected a Fellow at Magdalen College at Oxford. Albert Lewis burst into tears on reading the news in his son's telegram. Lewis immediately sent a letter to his father expressing his deep gratitude for six years of support. [16]

The Belfast *Times* on May 20, 1925, announced "Honor for Belfast Man." The newspaper noted that the new Oxford don was the son of "Mr. A. J. Lewis, the well-known Belfast solicitor."[17] That summer brought a rare, pleasant holiday in Ireland with his father.

Days of poverty for C. S. Lewis were over.

Chapter 6

"Too Much Straw and Not Enough Bricks"

Lewis took up residence in 1925 at Magdalen, one of the largest and most beautiful of the Oxford colleges. He retained his rooms on the second floor of the third stairwell of the New Building for the next twenty-nine years. New in name only, the building dated from 1793. On the east side of the building, a tree-lined path called Addison's Walk ran alongside a meadow. The path, named for essayist Joseph Addison, quickly became a favorite of Lewis.[1]

Deer grazed below the window of the big sitting room of his apartment. The windows of a smaller sitting room and the bedroom looked out on Magdalen's main buildings and the tower beyond. Lewis made a ritual of climbing the tower every May Day and often took guests to the top.[2]

Meals came as part of his stipend, but Oxford supplied no furniture. Lewis made haphazard choices about couch, chairs, table and carpet. Albert Lewis had noted his son's lack of interest in shopping, or going to the bank, or even getting a hair cut.[3]

Through the years, students came to the room filled with well-worn furniture, books and papers. Lewis was usually wearing rumpled flannel trousers, a brown tweed jacket, and worn carpet slippers. Warren observed that his brother could make a new suit look shabby by the second time he wore it.[4]

Lewis sat in a large overstuffed chair with his ever-present pipe. Bright eyes and ruddy cheeks made him appear more like a farmer than an Oxford don. But scholars who sat in the chair opposite Lewis to read their essays knew the formidable intellect they faced. Lewis listened with notebook in hand while they presented their opinions on the assigned subject.[5]

His responses followed Kirkpatrick's pattern. A well-written piece brought "There is a good deal in what you say." Mediocrity received "There is something in what you say." Serious problems were indicated with "There *may* be something in what you say." Wordy texts with little proof prompted "Too much straw and not enough bricks." If a student had been overzealous in making a point, Lewis advised, "Not with Brogans, please, slippers are in order when you proceed to make a literary point." Praise came sparingly in the form of "Much of that was very well said." Years later, a former student flashed back to student days when Lewis commented on a grammar point, "Great snakes, you can't do that."[6]

He was a creature of habit who disliked interruption. He disdained technology, refused to drive a car, and found the telephone particularly annoying.

Nothing, however, seemed to interrupt his thoughts. A student once halted his essay mid-sentence when the telephone rang. Lewis spoke for several minutes then returned. He repeated the student's partial sentence exactly so that he could continue reading.[7]

Lewis made sure each student got a full hour. Sometimes it was a struggle to fill the time. When there was nothing else to say about the essay, Lewis moved to some subject he thought might interest the student. This left some tongue-tied in the presence of his powerful personality. Many students found him reserved. He had little personal contact with students and even had trouble distinguishing those who came in pairs. Others, like Roger Lancelyn Green and Alan Griffiths, later known as Dom Bede Griffiths, became lifelong friends.[8]

During the 1940s women scholars came in pairs. He treated them with courteous formality as they read and discussed each other's essays. One young woman from a rural area felt woefully out of place in her worn scholar's gown. Her partner, an attractive, wealthier young woman, suggested that they not be harsh on each other's papers. After letting her partner's essay pass without criticism, she was stunned by the scathing remarks made about her own. She fumbled for a response, saying she could make no further defense. Lewis boomed out, "Well, I can!" "How he demolished the attack on me I do not remember, but his kindness and support I shall never forget."[9]

Lewis insisted that his students understand the language of the time when an author's work appeared. He took them back to Greek and Latin texts to show how these authors influenced the medieval literature he taught. To help them understand the influence of Old

English, he instituted spirited "Beer and Beowulf" evenings.[10]

As part of his duties, Lewis gave lectures. He expected few people to attend the first one, but the room overflowed. His reputation grew until he became the most popular lecturer at Oxford. People sat on the window sills when the big hall at Magdalen was full. Even with serious subjects, he included humorous, unexpected examples. He pulled quotations from his tremendous knowledge of literature. Often these quotes were in their original language.[11]

He entered the lecture room with black robe flowing and began speaking before he got to the lectern. He spoke slowly enough for students to take notes. His own lecture notes went unused. When finished, he folded up the notes and walked out the door. One of his students summed it up, "His lectures were meaty . . . points were clearly enumerated; arguments beautifully articulated; illustrations richly chosen."[12]

For a person so widely read, he owned few books. On his bookshelf he kept books by St. Thomas Aquinas and a copy of *Beowulf*. He also had books written by his friend Charles Williams. Children's books included Owen Barfield's *The Silver Trumpet* and J.R.R. Tolkien's *The Hobbit*. But his own books were missing. He gave those away.[13]

He used the Bodleian for his reading. He discovered Duke Humphrey's Library very soon after coming to Oxford. It had been established with the duke's donations in the fifteenth century. Lewis found a secluded area between shelves where he could work. A little window looked out on a garden below. To his sorrow, it was never opened. But he could leave books on the table at the end of the day and find them waiting when he returned. He felt everything would have been perfect if only he had a soft chair and could smoke.[14]

With a command of Greek, Latin, French, Italian, Old English, and some knowledge of German, he read sources in their original language. He became upset with history writers who slanted their accounts. When Lewis read the writings of people who lived at a particular time, he often formed a different idea from the one presented by the historians.[15]

Research became a challenge. There seemed to be no starting point for a subject. Invariably, he needed to know something else first. Perhaps, he suggested, the only starting point was the Biblical words "In the beginning . . . "[16]

Lewis was happy among books, but unfortunately college faculty were required to help run the college. Lewis lasted only one year of a two-year term as vice-president. His phenomenal memory for quotations did not extend to everyday life. He forgot to record meeting room reservations. More than once, two groups arrived to find they were scheduled at the same time.[17]

Life at Magdalen followed a pattern much like student days. He woke up at 7:15 and had a cup of tea. Chapel was at 8:00. A notoriously fast eater, he had breakfast in the Common Room from 8:15 to 8:25. Returning to his room, he wrote letters until 9:00 when his first pupil arrived. Four hours later, he went home to have lunch with the Moores. After a long walk, he had tea and then returned to Oxford for more tutoring between 5:00 and 7:00 P.M. Dinner was at 7:15. He spent evenings reading or attending meetings of literary groups like the Martlets or the Socratic Club which he had helped found. Tuesdays were his "Beer and Beowulf." On Thursday nights for many years, close friends known as the Inklings met in his apartment.[18]

During his years at Oxford, Lewis's reputation grew as he lectured and wrote both scholarly and popular books. Nights during the week were spent at his Oxford apartment. On weekends he disappeared to a separate world, two miles away.

CHAPTER 7

"As Good as an Extra Maid"

From his early days as a student at Oxford, Lewis had maintained a home with Janie Moore and her daughter Maureen. To Mrs. Moore, he became the son she had lost. Lewis, who called her "Minto," spoke of her as his mother.[1]

Her mothering role began with her siblings when she was quite young. If anyone had the slightest hint of illness, she brought out the thermometer. She loved to cook and kept a large garden. She canned fruit and gave it away. They raised chickens. Lewis joked that the best place for a chicken was on the table. Even after he became famous, Mrs. Moore assigned him chores. He was, she said, "as good as an extra maid."[2]

They kept cats and dogs. One dog named Mr. Papworth refused to eat if anyone looked at him. Lewis took him for walks, throwing the dog's food over his shoulder. If Lewis turned around, the dog stopped eating.[3]

Albert Lewis disapproved of his son's involvement with Mrs. Moore. In spite of the rift between them, Lewis wrote weekly to his father about life at the university and the books he was reading. Visits to Ireland to see his father, however, were uneasy. In 1927, their last holiday together was a pleasant one. Warren was there, too. "Roses all the way," Albert Lewis wrote in his diary.[4]

Two years later, Albert was dying of cancer. Warren was serving in China, and Lewis went to Ireland to care for his father. That summer at Little Lea profoundly affected him. He saw his father's courage and sunny spirit during his final days.[5] After his father seemed to improve, Lewis hurried back to Oxford to start the 1929 school term, only to be called back.

Funeral arrangements made him see his father in light of Lewis family traditions. Tedious conversations with his uncles contrasted with his father's lively and interesting personality. Lewis sat in the silent house where he had felt such resentment. "Now you could do anything on earth you cared to in the study at midday or on Sunday, and it is beastly."[6]

At the end of the academic year, Lewis took Mrs. Moore to Belfast to help him sort through the furnishings so that Little Lea could be put up for sale. Family papers went into a big chest. Book dealers culled good editions from mounds of novels. The piano was sold. Albert Lewis's collection of bowler hats went to dealers in Oxford. Lewis had to dispose of his mother's clothing because his father had never done that. For himself and Warren, he set aside two hall chairs from their great grandfather's house in Wales, book cases, the grandfather clock, the phonograph, the telescope, and the microscope.[7]

Warren asked especially that his brother find his illustrated *Mother Goose*. He also suggested that they preserve the toys from the "little end room" and create another special place for them. Lewis objected. Nothing could ever match their childhood memory. In the end, the two brothers took the unopened chest of Boxen characters, dug a hole in the garden, and buried it.[8]

As a last act, the brothers placed a memorial window in St. Mark's, the Belfast church where their Grandfather Hamilton had baptized them. The middle saint of the three-panel window honoring Albert and Flora Lewis holds a chalice very similar to the silver one the Lewis family gave the church in 1908 in honor of Albert's father.[9]

Warren Lewis's army career had taken him far away to France, West Africa, and China, but Little Lea had always been home. Lewis insisted that his brother come to Oxford.

The brothers were very similar. Both were stocky with broad faces. Both enjoyed smoking their pipes, drinking beer, and taking long walks through the countryside. Their nickname for each other was "Piggibuddy" or "P.B." It came from a nanny who had threatened to spank their piggybottoms.[10]

Although Warren Lewis had no university training, he was extremely well-read. Their letters were filled with book discussions. On one occasion, Lewis discovered a book containing Warren's notes alongside the text. It seemed to him that his brother was standing there talking to him.[11]

Warren had liked machines. He owned a motorcycle with a sidecar. During World War II, he lived on his motorboat and patrolled the Upper Thames river.[12]

The Marion E. Wade Center, at the edge of the Wheaton College campus in Wheaton, Illinois, has a large collection of C. S. Lewis's books and papers that were donated to the center by Warren Lewis.

Both brothers enjoyed eating. On a trip to a club in 1924, they dined on fish, cutlets with green peas, a large serving of strawberries and cream. The evening included a tankard of local beer. Unfortunately, Warren Lewis became an alcoholic. He periodically retreated to a monastery in Ireland to recover from binge episodes.[13]

In 1932 the newspaper carried the announcement of Warren's retirement after eighteen years in the army. He felt the time had been a good trade-off. At forty, he was now free to "begin the business of living."[14]

With money from the sale of Little Lea, the Lewis brothers joined with Mrs. Moore in 1930 to purchase nine acres in Headington Quarry. The property had once been the site of a brick factory. Two brick kilns gave the house its name. Water came from a spring on the property. Fred Paxford, gardener at the Kilns for thirty-four years, credited the water for his good eyesight at age seventy.

A lake about 100 yards long and 40 yards wide had formed in the pit where clay had been dug. It was full of fish, and Lewis swam there. About half the property was wooded. Lewis loved the animals, especially the rabbits. He refused to let any trees be cut.[15]

During university sessions, Warren Lewis occupied the smaller bedroom of his brother's apartment at Magdalen College. Intelligent and likeable, he did not have the dominating personality of his younger brother, but he maintained an interest in world affairs. It appalled him that Lewis did not read the newspaper. Lewis contended that if he really needed to know something, somebody would tell him.[16]

During Warren's army service, he learned to type. After leaving the army, he spent two years sorting through the mountainous Lewis and Hamilton family papers. As he arranged and typed them, he discarded original documents. He had several thousand typed sheets bound into eleven volumes titled *Memoirs of the Lewis Family 1850-1930*. Commonly known as the *Lewis Papers*, they are now housed in the research collection at the Marion C. Wade Center in Wheaton, Illinois.[17]

As C. S. Lewis's fame grew, so did his correspondence. He answered all letters, writing in tiny script, often on scraps of paper. Warren began to type the letters to relieve him of some of the work. Warren numbered them in sequence, showing the year and the number of the letter.[18]

Warren Lewis resented Mrs. Moore's demands on his famous brother. He called her a tyrant, but he took part in planting trees at the Kilns. The brothers referred to this as "public works."[19]

Young people lived at the Kilns during World War II to escape air raids in London. They found Mrs. Moore to be kind and very caring. When they arrived, they had no idea that the rumpled person called "Jack" was the well-known Oxford professor. To Lewis's merriment, one mistook him for the gardener.[20]

> [Lewis] answered all letters, writing in tiny script, often on scraps of paper.

In the evenings Lewis discussed school work with them. When a mentally challenged boy arrived, Lewis made flash cards. He worked each night trying to teach the boy to read. On Sunday afternoons, Warren Lewis played symphonies on the phonograph with its large wooden speaker. He was the only one allowed to touch it.[21]

Jill Flewett, called June, stayed for only a short period but left behind her food ration card. Mrs. Moore sent a dozen eggs each month to the Flewett family in London. In 1943 sixteen-year-old Jill came back for a holiday and stayed two years. Mrs. Moore was in her seventies and frail. Jill's duties included feeding twenty-five hens and thirty rabbits.[22]

When she left, Lewis wrote her, "Oh what a sad waking up this morning. . . . Tell June that the hens were asking for her first thing this morning . . . that Warnie is even more depressed than usual; that the cats, under this shared calamity, sank their common differences . . . . We are the ghost and ruin of a house."[23]

Jill wanted to be an actress. While she lived at the Kilns, Lewis took her to a Shakespeare play. Two of his students were appearing in it, as was future movie star Richard Burton. Lewis paid for Jill's theater training, but she always felt his greatest gift to her was a feeling of self-worth. Lewis anonymously paid university expenses and vocational training for other evacuees as well.[24]

In one of the ironies of Lewis's life, Jill Flewett married Clement Freud, the grandson of psychoanalyst Sigmund Freud. One of Lewis's great controversies was with Freud's ideas about psychoanalysis.[25]

As the years went by, Mrs. Moore's health failed. She had trouble walking and her mind wandered. Lewis attended to her constantly. In 1941, he wrote to his friend Sister Penelope asking for prayers. "I can do so little for her." Several years later he wrote a raging letter of frustration to Barfield. "Things were never worse at the Kilns." He sent an apology a week later.[26]

Maureen Moore had married Leonard Blake, a music teacher at Malvern College. Sometimes they exchanged houses with the Lewis brothers while Maureen took care of her mother.[27]

After a bad fall, Mrs. Moore was confined to a nursing home. For nine months Lewis visited her every day until her death in January 1951. Warren Lewis felt relief when she died. Lewis was moved to write again to Sister Penelope a few months later. He needed prayers this time because things were too easy.[28]

The Kilns in Headington Quarry was only a short distance away from Magdalen College, Oxford, but it was a world away from the life C. S. Lewis lived there.

CHAPTER 8

"Has Nobody Got Anything to Read Us?"

At Oxford, Lewis surrounded himself with a close circle of friends with wits as sharp as his own. They gathered in Lewis's apartment for vigorous, late-night discussions.

Foremost among them was J. R. R. Tolkien. He was six years older than Lewis and, like most Englishmen of their age, had served in World War I. While recovering from a long, serious illness, he began writing *The Silmarillion*. This was the prehistory for his stories about Middle Earth. Like Lewis, Tolkien fell under the spell of Norse myths as a young person. He taught himself the Norse language so that he could read the original stories. He came to Oxford as professor of Anglo-Saxon the year Lewis began his Fellowship.[1]

It took three years for Lewis and Tolkien to discover their mutual interest. Lewis joined the Kolbitárs, a group that Tolkien formed to study Icelandic poetry. The name was a joke about men who lounged "so close to the fire in the winter that they bit the coal." Lewis "hammered" his way along when it was his turn to read. Just seeing the names of Norse gods and heroes rekindled the thrill he had known as a boy.[2]

Unknown to his colleagues, Tolkien had been creating a massive imaginary world of creatures who had their own language, history, and myths. When Tolkien finally showed Lewis his story about hobbits, Lewis was overwhelmed with the carefully created "subcreation" of myths and history. He immediately wrote Greeves that Tolkien could have been an equal partner in their youthful friendship. When The Hobbit was published, Lewis's review called it "exceptional." Tolkien was enormously grateful for Lewis's encouragement.[3]

It took another twelve years for Tolkien to finish *The Lord of the Rings*. When he read it, Warren Lewis could only say, "Golly, what a book!" C. S. Lewis's review described it as "lightning from a clear sky."[4]

Lewis and Tolkien met on Tuesday mornings at a pub called the Bird and Baby. It was commonly called Baby and Bird because the signboard featured an eagle carrying the infant Ganymede. They were joined by others for beer and lively discussion.[5]

On Thursday evenings the group called the Inklings gathered in Lewis's apartment. The name was a pun for people who had vague ideas and dabbled in ink.[6] There was no set membership—just extremely well-read men who enjoyed each other's company.

This group also formed Lewis's companions on week-long walking tours around England. They tramped cross-country about twenty miles a day, following maps to villages where they ate and lodged.

Serious conversation stopped at lunch. Afternoons were filled with banter.[7]

Warren Lewis's diary recorded some activities at Inklings meetings. The popularity of Lewis's religious books in the United States prompted Americans to send food during the rationing that followed World War II. Hams were supplied by a Maryland doctor. They covered canned goods with a sheet, and blindly chose a lump. They learned to leave large cans alone. These might be prunes. One package included a dinner jacket. It was too small for Lewis and was auctioned off. Tolkien's son Christopher, now an Inkling, got the jacket.[8]

On a typical evening, after the men brought out their pipes, Lewis would call out, "Well, has nobody got anything to read us?" After someone read a piece, they held lively

> ["Inklings"] was a pun for people who had vague ideas and dabbled in ink.

discussions, giving honest criticisms. Lewis observed that Tolkien would change nothing in his writings or would start over again.[9]

The meetings had no rules or agenda. One session debated the ethics of cannibalism. Another centered on ghosts. They discussed Shakespeare and hymns. Warren Lewis, who eventually wrote six books on French history, read some of his work.[10]

Sometimes they voted not to listen to a piece. When they vetoed Lewis's essay on "Chance," he pointed out that if they died that night they would never know about Chance. Warren responded, "Every cloud has a silver lining." When there was no topic to discuss, they spent the night joking and making puns. Tolkien wrote a tongue-in-cheek poem in Old English describing their deliberations and horseplay.[11]

Two of this diverse group, Neville Coghill and Owen Barfield, had entered Oxford with Lewis. Coghill, a fellow Irishman and a Kolbitar, was an expert on Geoffrey Chaucer and translated *The Canterbury Tales*.[12]

Owen Barfield earned the name "Second Friend" because he disagreed with Lewis over things they both liked. They had a long-running debate that they called the Great War. Barfield held an unorthodox view of Christianity called Anthroposophy, which Lewis could not accept. But Barfield's scholarly books were impressive. He believed that changes in language revealed the development of imagination through the ages. After he was called to London to work in his father's law office, he rarely attended. Barfield straightened out Lewis's finances and set up the charitable trust that handled Lewis's gifts.[13]

A. C. Harwood, although not an Inkling, was dubbed "Lord of the Walks" for his enthusiasm for the walking tours. He and his wife Daphne were members of the same English folk dance society as the Owen Barfields. Lewis dedicated *Miracles* to them, and one of their sons was Lewis's godchild.[14]

Henry V. D. Dyson, nicknamed Hugo, was an Inkling who read widely but wrote little. He had an immense knowledge of Shakespeare and rattled off appropriate quotations for any situation. Dyson preferred to talk. Lewis described one session where he was a "roaring cataract of nonsense." Dyson's interruptions were so maddening to Tolkien that he eventually stopped reading.[15]

Dr. R. E. Havard, called Humphry, was invited to

an Inklings meeting after he treated Lewis for influenza. Havard earned the nickname U.Q. (Useless Quack) when he failed to show up to give Warren Lewis a ride.[16]

Charles Williams, an editor at the Oxford University Press, joined the group when the press moved from London during the air raids. Finances had forced Williams to drop out of college, but he could quote more authors than even Lewis. He wrote poetry, supernatural fiction, dramas, literary criticism, and religious essays. His work was mystical and hard to understand. At one Inklings meeting Lewis said Williams had been "unusually intelligible."[17]

With Lewis's help, Williams was allowed to lecture at Oxford. The faculty considered him unqualified because he had no university degree. His lectures on poet John Milton were highly successful. When Williams died suddenly in 1945, Lewis acknowledged his debt to this "friend of friends." Tolkien, however, disliked the occult in Williams's writing. Tolkien believed that devils were real.[18]

During 1946, Inklings meetings were well attended. That year Tolkien read parts of *The Lord of the Rings* almost every week. But three years later, Warren recorded in his diary, "No one turned up after dinner." A week later the chairs were empty again. Meetings at the Bird and Baby continued, but there were no more Inklings gatherings.[19]

The friendship between Tolkien and Lewis waned. One reason may have been Lewis's close relationship with Charles Williams. The other major factor was the entrance of a woman named Joy Gresham into C. S. Lewis's life.

Chapter 9

"I Never Thought to Have..."

The book title *Surprised by Joy* came to have a marvelous double meaning in Lewis's life. At twenty-two he had described marriage as a "fatal tomb" for interesting men.[1] His marriage to Helen Joy Davidman Gresham at fifty-eight surprised his friends, his brother, and most of all himself.

Joy was born in New York City in 1915 of Jewish parents who had come from the Ukraine. They not did practice their religion, and at age eight, Joy announced that she was an atheist. An avid reader and a poet, she earned a Master of Arts degree in English Literature from Columbia University. She participated in the Communist movement. Her poetry book, *Letters to a Comrade*, won the Yale Series of Younger Poets Award in 1938.[2]

She married successful author William Lindsay

Gresham. He was alcoholic, but they lived comfortably on earnings from *Nightmare Alley*, his book that became a movie. Their two sons, David and Douglas, were still quite young when Gresham's drinking became so bad that he sought help. This led the couple to join the Presbyterian church.[3]

Still, the marriage was troubled. Joy had been impressed when she read Lewis's books. In 1952 she planned a trip to England, hoping to meet him. He invited her to Oxford.[4]

Lewis's friends were aghast at this abrupt, uninhibited woman. Lewis was fascinated by a mind that "sprang and knocked you over before you knew what was happening."[5]

Separation failed to help the Gresham marriage. They agreed to a divorce. Joy and her sons moved to England in the winter of 1953. During a four-day visit to the Kilns, the boys' antics left the two bachelors breathless.[6]

At this time, Joy finished writing *Smoke on the Mountain*, a contemporary discussion of the Ten Commandments. Lewis contributed the forward.[7]

In 1954, after nearly thirty years at Oxford, Lewis resigned. By this time he had published a number of religious books. Their tremendous popularity offended many faculty members. They refused to give him a professorship. Magdalene College, Cambridge, on the other hand, was delighted to have Lewis take up residency as Professor of Medieval and Renaissance English. A year later his old University College at Oxford gave him an Honorary Fellowship, but Lewis remained at Cambridge until he retired.[8]

At Cambridge his new college was again Magdalene, spelled with an "e" but still pronounced MAUD-lin like the Oxford one. Lewis joked that he was glad to remain under the protection of this Biblical "lady" who seemed to know him well.[9]

Teaching at Cambridge was a pleasure. He no longer tutored. He was free to write and give lectures. His inaugural lecture, given on his fifty-sixth birthday, was called *"De Descriptione Temporum."* In it he called himself a dinosaur because of his literary views.[10]

Even after moving to Cambridge, Lewis continued to return to the Kilns on weekends. Meetings at the Bird and Baby were changed to Monday so that he could attend on his "free" day. He then returned to Cambridge on the evening train.[11]

Joy had been in England a couple of years when the British government refused to renew her visa. To keep her from being deported, Lewis married her in a civil ceremony at the Oxford registry office on April 23, 1956. There was no announcement. Lewis did not consider them married because the ceremony had not been performed by a clergyman.[12]

Joy was having severe pain in her leg. What doctors first thought was rheumatism turned out to be cancer. It had eaten through one thigh bone and had spread to her other leg and shoulder. Death was a matter of time. Lewis wanted to bring her to the Kilns, but he would not do that until they had a religious ceremony. Several Anglican ministers refused to perform the marriage because Joy was divorced. Then, on March 21, 1957, Reverend Peter Bide stood at Joy's bedside and heard their vows. A small notice appeared in the paper.[13]

By May of the next year, Joy seemed to recover. She supervised renovations at the Kilns. They joked that bookcases were holding up the walls. She planted gardens. At a belated reception Lewis remarked to two friends, "I never thought to have at sixty what passed me by in my twenties."[14]

Warren Lewis, so resentful of Mrs. Moore, admired Joy's courage. Pain had not dulled her sense of humor. She shared his interest in French history, and her wide-ranging conversations captivated him. He planned to move, but both insisted that he stay.[15]

As Joy's health improved, Lewis's declined. He developed osteoporosis, a bone-loss disease. She was able to walk with a cane. He wore a back brace. Lewis considered it a good trade-off.[16]

They were able to take a vacation to Ireland in 1958. Soon afterwards, Joy's cancer returned. Lewis's former pupil Roger Lancelyn Green and his wife planned a trip to Greece. Joy was eager to go, too. In spite of her pain, she and Lewis climbed the Parthenon in Athens in the spring of 1960.[17]

Three months later she died. They spent the last evening playing Scrabble and reading a play together. The next morning her screams awoke them. She died that night at the hospital.[18]

Lewis handled his grief in the only manner he knew—with his pen. He filled four small notebooks with journal-like entries that chronicled his anguish. "No one ever told me that grief felt so much like fear . . . . I keep on swallowing." Sudden jabs of "red-hot memory" struck him down.[19]

A Grief Observed was published in 1961 with N. W. Clerk listed as author. The lost love is identified only as H, a reference to Joy's first name. Lewis never spoke of the book, but it was not hard to identify the author.[20]

Lewis's health continued to decline. In July 1963, he had a heart attack. Maureen Moore Blake, who had inherited a title and a castle from a distant relative, came to see him in the hospital. He had not recognized anyone all that day. She stood by Lewis's bed and said,

"Jack, it's Maureen." He corrected her. "No, it's Lady Dunbar of Hempriggs." She could not believe that he remembered. Lewis responded, "How could *I* forget a fairy tale?"[21]

Lewis recovered enough to go home, but he did not count that a blessing. He noted that he, like the Biblical Lazarus, had to die all over again. He did not fear dying, but he was grieved to cancel his trip to Ireland. "Oh, Arthur, never to see you again."[22]

Books were his solace. Shortly before his death he invited a friend to come talk with him about *Les Laisions Dangereuses*. "Wow, what a book!" He continued to write letters until the day he died.[23]

The end came on November 22, 1963, but the world paid little attention. That was the day that President John F. Kennedy was assassinated.

The announcement of Lewis's death did not appear in the paper in time for many to attend his funeral that cold clear day. Maureen Blake and her husband joined Douglas Gresham, George Sayer, and Fred Paxford at the service. After it was over, Lewis's casket bearing one candle was carried out from the Headington Quarry church and buried in the churchyard.[24]

J. R. R. Tolkien and his son Christopher were there as well. Although their friendship was no longer close, Tolkien felt a deep loss. He wrote his daughter that the death of several friends had made him feel like a tree losing its leaves but that Lewis's death was "an axe-blow to the roots." To another son, he wrote of Lewis, "He was a great man of whom the cold-blooded official obituaries only scraped the surface."[25]

Warren could not bring himself to attend the funeral. Later, he placed on his brother's marker the quotation that Albert Lewis had put on their mother's grave.

"Men must endure their going hence."[26]

CHAPTER 10

"It Is Always Better to Read Chaucer Again..."

It was soon after Lewis accepted the position at Cambridge that the Milton Society of America held an evening honoring him as an authority on John Milton. Lewis did not attend, but he sent a letter thanking them. He noted that his books were "a mixed bag."[1] Indeed they are—scholarly works, science fiction novels, children's fantasies, and books on Christian themes. He often worked on these simultaneously.

Very few drafts of Lewis manuscripts remain. Unlike Tolkien, who worked slowly and made many revisions, Lewis worked quickly. Friends noted his ability to speak well-organized thoughts extemporaneously. That same skill seemed to apply to his writing. On the other hand, the lack of drafts could mean that he threw them out. He did not keep letters. Tolkien complained that Lewis even threw away two manuscripts that belonged to him.[2]

Lewis, who began his literary career as a poet, published a long narrative poem in 1926 called *Dymer*. Friends thought *Dymer* was good, but it dropped from sight. He continued to write short poems that were published in *Punch* and *The Oxford Magazine*. He signed them "N.W.". The initials stood for Nat Whilk, an Old English term that meant "I know not whom."[3] Originally, he started as a poet, but it was his prose that made Lewis famous.

The idea for his first academic book came from reading the medieval texts he loved. Lewis wrote his father in 1928 that he had begun the first chapter of a book about medieval love poetry.[4] The vast resources of the Bodleian Library forced him to limit the subject to the time from early Middle Ages through the late Sixteen Century. Sitting in his favorite cubicle in the library, he became a master of the subject.

It took eight years to finish *The Allegory of Love: A Study in Medieval Tradition*. He dedicated the book to Owen Barfield. *The Allegory of Love* won the Gollancz Memorial Prize for Literature in 1937 and established Lewis's reputation as a literary scholar. In spite of its scholarly intent, *The Allegory of Love* was highly readable. One biographer commented, "Few books on what seems such a remote subject are such lively, general reading."[5]

The Allegory of Love became the standard for the study of medieval literature and revived interest in Edmund Spenser. Spenser's *Fairie Queen* was one of Lewis's favorite books. Later adding a fourth type of love to the three discussed in connection with Spenser, Lewis published *The Four Loves* in 1960.[6]

The manuscript of *The Allegory of Love* made a

tremendous impression when it reached the desk of Oxford University Press editor, Charles Williams. It happened that Lewis was reading Williams's book, *The Place of the Lion*, about the same time. As a result, the two men developed a close friendship.[7]

Williams' lectures on the poet John Milton led Lewis to develop a series on Milton himself. He presented these at Oxford and at University College, North Wales. The lectures were published in 1942 as *A Preface to "Paradise Lost."*[8]

When Williams died, Lewis and other Inklings honored him with *Essays Presented to Charles Williams*. Lewis wrote the preface for this book about writing and contributed the essay "On Stories."[9]

In 1954, a massive book that Lewis had worked on for twenty years was finally published. *English Literature in the Sixteenth Century, Excluding Drama* is volume III of *The Oxford History of English Literature*. A contemporary at Oxford observed Lewis pouring over manuscripts in the Bodleian with what seemed a wall of silence around himself. Watching him "moving steadily through some huge double-columned folio in his reading for his Oxford history was to have an object lesson in what concentration meant." Warren Lewis observed that his brother was one of those persons whose recreation overlapped with their vocation.[10]

The writing went on so long that Lewis, Tolkien and others had a private joke referring to the work as OHEL. Lewis's breezy 700-page volume is a classic. The authors included, many of them obscure, supported Lewis's belief that learning did not stop during the Middle Ages. He always avoided the word "Renaissance" and insisted instead that the Industrial

Revolution was the real dividing point in cultural history.[11]

In 1964, the year after Lewis's death, *The Discarded Image: An Introduction into Medieval and Renaissance Literature* was published. Much of the book had been worked out in lectures he presented called "Prolegomena to Medieval Literature" and "Prolegomena to Renaissance Literature." Lewis urged readers to understand the world as people in the Middle Ages saw it, at the time when the earth was considered to be the center of the universe.[12]

Lewis wrote other books on criticism. *An Experiment in Criticism* (1961) stated his preference to read himself what an author had written, rather than what someone said about the work. "It is always better to read Chaucer again than to read a new criticism of him."[13]

Lewis had a phenomenal memory. He had a habit of hand-indexing his books. Sometimes he played a game with guests. They chose a series of numbers that stood for a bookcase in the room, a shelf, a book, and a page. The guest was directed to find the book and read a random line on the chosen page. Lewis not only named the book but usually quoted the rest of the page.[14]

Studies in Words called on that vast memory. In it, Lewis traced the evolution of words. He warned about the danger of interpreting old texts using only the modern meanings. Philologist Lewis, lover of books, knew where the words came from.[15]

Chapter 11

"Pseudo-Bunyan's Periplus"

Lewis's life made a full circle before he started writing religious books. He was born into a family steeped in the Church of Ireland, and his tutor Annie Harper taught him about Heaven. His mother's death, however, was traumatic for him. He soon rejected religion altogether. He read myths for pleasure, but he accepted only science as real.[1]

Lewis's training with Kirkpatrick and his study of philosophy convinced him that he should be able to prove everything by rational thinking. At Oxford, he encountered the occult when he visited mystic poet William Butler Yeats, but rejected that. What surprised him was that his friend Neville Coghill, a brilliant student, turned out to be a Christian.[2]

Lewis faced a dilemma when he started teaching Carritt's philosophy classes. He needed some standard for ultimate truth. He chose the term "Spirit" but gave it no religious meaning. Then he was thoroughly shaken by the Christian view of history in G. K. Chesterton's *The Everlasting Man*. While riding a bus in 1929, he suddenly faced a choice—to accept or reject the idea of a supreme being. He compared his feeling at the moment he accepted the idea that there was a God to that of a melting snowman as his old ideas seemed to dissolve.[3]

Still, he struggled against the idea that God should control his life. He dismissed Christianity as a religion for simple minds. Then in September 1931, after dinner in his apartment with Tolkien and Dyson, the talk centered on myths. They continued their discussion into the early hours of the morning while circling Addison's Walk. Tolkien, a devout Catholic, characterized the story of Jesus as a "dying god" myth. Lewis shared Tolkien's belief that all myths held truth. The difference in this story, Tolkien said, was that God was the author and the people were real. Suddenly, Lewis's last barrier to Christianity disappeared.[4]

A week later, while riding in the sidecar of Warren's motorcycle on the way to Whipsnade Zoo, Lewis decided to rejoin the church. At the zoo, they stopped at the bear's cage. They named him Bultitude. The bear became special to Lewis that day. He wrote Warren about seeing Bultitude on other visits. A bear named Mr. Bultitude appears in *That Hideous Strength*.[5]

For the first time in twenty years, Lewis took communion on Christmas Day 1931. Unknown to him, Warren, half a world away in Shanghai, China, did that same thing that day.[6] Not long afterward, Lewis began to write his religious books.

Lewis was not a typical church member. He disliked church services but went to Chapel each day because he felt he should. He preferred private devotions. He poured out his struggle to live a Christian life in letters to Sister Penelope, an Anglican nun at St. Mary the Virgin at Wantage. They began exchanging letters after she read one of his books, and these continued until his death.[7]

Lewis dismissed hymns as sentimental poetry. He thought most church architecture was ugly. But, even as an atheist, he found Wells Cathedral interesting. With its many builders over the centuries, it became an "age made into stone." On the other hand, towering Salisbury Cathedral, built from one plan, was a "petrified moment . . . thousands of tons of masonry held in place by an idea, a religion." At the time he wrote those words, he considered them both useless.[8]

> [The] moment he accepted the idea that there was a God . . . his old ideas seemed to melt away.

Lewis was deeply concerned when churches used doctrine to justify actions that he considered counter to God's ways. His nine-year correspondence in Latin with Don Giovanni Calabria, a Roman Catholic priest in Verona, spoke against the intolerance on both sides of the Protestant-Catholic dispute in Ireland.[9]

Lewis communicated his understanding of faith and moral ethics in books, sermons, and essays. His first religious book, *The Pilgrim's Regress*, was an allegory suggested by John Bunyan's *Pilgrim's Progress*. Its title indicates Lewis's return to Christianity. He struggled to write it as poetry but changed to prose and completed it during a two-week visit with Greeves in the summer of 1932.[10] It was published the following year.

Originally, Lewis expected only his university friends to read the book. The subtitle read: *Pseudo-Bunyan's Periplus; An Allegorical Apology for Christianity, Reason, and Romanticism.* The Greek word periplus means "circular voyage." Wisely, that part of the subtitle was removed. One reader still found the book difficult. Lewis advised her not to bother—it was his first religious book and he did not know how to make things simple.[11]

The book jabs at Sigmund Freud by giving the name Sigmund Enlightenment to the jailor. Lewis later wrote specifically about his distrust of psychologists, who, he believed, forced their own ideas on patients.[12]

Early in 1940 he published *The Problem of Pain.* The book is dedicated to the Inklings. Lewis put forth the idea that suffering results when humans use their free will to choose evil. He called pain a "megaphone" that God uses to get our attention. Dr. Havard, who wrote the medical appendix in the book, kept quoting passages to Lewis when he had the mumps.[13]

As war raged in Europe, a Royal Air Force chaplain invited Lewis to speak to pilots who faced death with each mission. Lewis learned to adapt to a different audience and traveled throughout England speaking at military posts. He refused to wear a robe and would not take pay on the grounds that he was not a theologian.[14]

In the jittery time when England expected to be invaded, the head of the British Broadcasting Company (BBC) asked Lewis to present a series of broadcasts to help citizens cope. For five weeks from August to

September 1941, he gave several fifteen-minute live broadcasts on the topic "Right and Wrong: A Clue to the Meaning of the Universe." His clear, resonant baritone voice and common sense ideas were perfect for the task.[15]

A second series, "What Christians Believe," aired in January and February 1942. The third, "Christian Behavior," was broadcast that Fall. A final series in early 1944 was called "Beyond Personality: The Christian View of God." The broadcasts were originally printed in three small booklets that were later published together in 1952 as *Mere Christianity*.[16]

Some listeners, such as TV personality Alistair Cooke, found Lewis's ideas simplistic. For others, the messages of personal responsibility in *Mere Christianity* brought powerful responses.[17]

Fifteen years after Lewis's death, Charles Colson was overwhelmed by *Mere Christianity*. Colson, adviser to President Richard Nixon, served prison time for his part in the illegal Watergate break-in that cost Nixon the presidency. After reading Lewis's essay, "The Humanitarian Theory of Punishment," Colson founded Prison Fellowship to help prisoners and their families understand justice. Lewis believed that crimes deserved punishment, but punishment should never be used as a deterrent to crime. This idea appeared again as part of the discussion in *The Abolition of Man*, published in 1943.[18]

As powerful as *Mere Christianity* was, *The Screwtape Letters* (1942) was a blockbuster. The idea of showing temptation from the devil's viewpoint came to Lewis as he left a church service. The Under Secretary to "Our Father Below" sends letters of advice and warning to Wormwood, a young novice with a new Christian "patient." Although he wrote the book quickly, Lewis found the writing distasteful—"dust, grit, thirst, and itch."[19]

Lewis believed that temptation was real. He presented the devil with "all the sharp know-how of the slipperiest salesman of a very large organization." Lewis dedicated *The Screwtape Letters* to Tolkien "in payment of a great debt." Charles Williams wrote a tongue-in-cheek review in the language of Screwtape. He called the book "dangerous" and signed the review Snigsozzle.[20]

One minister, however, labeled *The Screwtape Letters* "diabolical" and canceled his subscription to

> ## The publication of *The Screwtape Letters* made Lewis famous on both sides of the Atlantic.

The Guardian when it appeared serially. But the public loved the book, and it is still in print. The publication of the American edition in 1943 made Lewis famous on both sides of the Atlantic. He appeared on the cover of *Time* magazine. Letters poured in, and Lewis painstakingly answered them all.[21]

The Great Divorce: A Dream, published in 1945, expresses Lewis's belief that choices determine eternal fate. A busload of quarrelsome people from hell are on their way to a holiday in paradise. Although greeted by cheerful residents of Heaven, all the riders except one refuse to enter because they are consumed by jealousy, vanity, or selfishness. Lewis shocked some readers by including a few real people. Tolkien was not impressed when he heard the story read at an Inklings meeting. He preferred Warren Lewis's well-researched and "wittily written" book about the court of French King Louis XIV.[22]

Miracles states Lewis's belief that supernatural forces can supercede the laws of nature. The book's third chapter brought sharp disagreement from G. E. M. Anscombe, a Catholic philosopher. She read a paper at a meeting of the Socratic Club in 1948. Lewis took his usual role of presenting a rebuttal. Anscombe was one of the few persons who ever argued Lewis to a standstill. He revised the chapter.[23]

Lewis's autobiography, *Surprised by Joy: The Shape of My Early Life*, was published in 1955. It is dedicated to Bede Griffiths. The book traces Lewis's journey to Christianity and his search for the feeling that he called Joy.

Lewis's fame in the United States led the Episcopal Radio-TV Foundation in Atlanta, Georgia, to ask for recordings. In 1958 the crew came to London to make tapes to broadcast in America. The messages contained clear, simple concepts combined with interesting illustrations and humor. A technician became so engrossed at one point in what Lewis was saying that he let the tape run out.[24]

The talks focused on four kinds of love—*Storge* (affection), *Philia* (friendship such as Lewis had with Greeves), *Eros* (physical love), and *Agape* (divine love that seeks good for others). Lewis pointed out that the first three were not appropriate at all times, but *Agape* could always be practiced.[25]

Lewis acted on this concept by setting up a charitable fund to receive two-thirds of his earnings. Contributions to individuals and to groups like the widows of clergymen were done anonymously. In typical Lewis fashion, he called the fund Agapargyry (love + money).[26]

Reflections on the Psalms was published in 1958 as an aid to personal meditation. Lewis loved the beautiful words of the Psalms. He considered Psalm 19 to be one of the greatest lyrics in the world and enjoyed the Hebrew-alphabet organization for Psalm 119.

His work on the Psalms led to an invitation to help revise the Psalter for the Church of England. Also serving on the committee was T. S. Eliot. In his early years, Lewis had expressed contempt for Eliot and other writers of modern poetry. He had come to respect Eliot by the time they worked together on this project. *The Revised Psalter* was published three years after Lewis's death.[27]

Publication of Lewis's books continued even though he was gone. *Letters to Malcolm, Chiefly on Prayer* was published in 1964. Walter Hooper, who served as Lewis's secretary during that last summer, has collected and edited numerous sermons, essays, and letters.

Chapter 12

"Nothing in Nature Is Quite Regular"

Lewis began writing science fiction for adults after remarking to Tolkien, "If they won't write the kind of books we want to read, we shall have to write them ourselves." Lewis then produced three space travel books. Tolkien never finished his own time travel story.[1]

Readers of Lewis's science fiction books notice several names such as Numinor that are very similar to those Tolkien used. Tolkien did not think this plagiarism. Lewis expected Tolkien to publish the stories he heard at Inklings meetings, but they had not been finished. Other names are Lewis's own. He created them by moving syllables around and listening for a sound that gave the emotion he wanted.[2]

It is not unusual that Lewis chose space travel for his science fiction books. Planets and stars fascinated him. He loved the night sky. Paxford, who sometimes drove Lewis to the observatory, was sorry that Lewis did not live to see men walk on the moon.[3]

Lewis had been reading H. G. Wells's stories since childhood, but David Lindsay's *Voyage to Arcturus* gave him the idea of combining science with the supernatural. Lewis made no effort to make the science in his stories correct. A character in *That Hideous Strength* remarks that "nothing in nature is *quite* regular."[4]

He developed his space trilogy after a pupil remarked that planets could be colonized. Lewis was horrified. He feared that evil would spread from this world to places where it had never been.[5]

The books are not allegories, but the theme of the struggle between good and evil saturates Lewis's fiction. In his science fiction series Lewis takes it one step further by having good come from evil. Scientists who wish to control mankind unknowingly set in motion events that bring Deep Heaven down to earth to vanquish evil. It amused Lewis that most readers were unaware that he was "smuggling" religion into their reading.[6]

Symbolism starts with the name of the main character, Dr. Elwin Ransom, a philologist. Tolkien's daughter thought that Ransom was a portrait of her father.[7] In the first book, *Out of the Silent Planet*, evil scientists kidnap Ransom. A rocket whisks him to Malacandra (Mars) where he meets the supreme ruler. The ruler asks what has happened on Thulcandra (Earth) since its "bent" ruler was forced out of heaven.

After reading *Out of the Silent Planet* in 1938, Sister Penelope invited Lewis to speak at the Anglican convent at Wantage. In his acceptance letter, an amused Lewis remarked about the odd tasks that God assigns. He joked, "The doors do open outwards as well, I trust?"[8] *Perelandra*, the second book in the trilogy, was published in 1943 and dedicated to "some ladies at Wantage."

Perelandra explores the idea of what would have happened had Adam and Eve not eaten from the forbidden tree in the Garden of Eden.[9] A casket-like spaceship takes Ransom to *Perelandra* (Venus) where two inhabitants live in peace. The evil scientist (Un-man) arrives. Ransom engages Un-Man in a long debate then kills him after a tremendous fight.

Lewis called the third book, *That Hideous Strength*, an adult fairy tale. It has magicians, devils, talking animals, and angels. A government agency called N.I.C.E (National Institute of Co-ordinated Experiments) performs experiments on animals. Evil forces plan to destroy the natural world, conquer death, and allow man to be his own god.

Lewis lampoons university foibles with the bickering college faculty. He honors Kirkpatrick in the skeptic MacPhee. He also shows his disapproval of experimenting on animals. Lewis wrote a pamphlet for the New England Anti-Vivisection Society. He believed that the only acceptable experiments on laboratory animals were humane ones that would help cure diseases.[10]

Lewis's fourth novel for adults turns to the story of Cupid and Psyche. *Till We Have Faces: A Myth Retold* was published in 1956, the year he married Joy Gresham. The book is dedicated to her. David Gresham saw his mother's influence in the creation of Orual, the homely sister who keeps her face covered. Lewis felt this was his best fiction. Many scholars agree that Orual is his most complex character. The public, however, did not like the book.[11]

CHAPTER 13

"Aslan Came Bounding Into It"

Lewis wrote seven fantasies for children. He called them fairy tales. The author commented, "I am not quite sure what made me, in a particular year of my life, feel that not only a fairy tale, but a fairy tale addressed to children, was exactly what I must write—or burst."[1]

The first book, *The Lion, the Witch, and the Wardrobe*, was published in 1950. Roger Lancelyn Green met with him almost weekly that year to read and offer suggestions on the books. All were finished by 1952, but they were published one a year. Green named them *The Chronicles of Narnia*.[2]

Pauline Baynes was chosen as illustrator because of pictures she had created for a Tolkien book. Lewis liked her work but was dismayed when he saw a knight with his shield on the wrong arm.[3]

In each story, good struggles against evil, but Lewis did not start out with a religious theme in mind. Then, "Aslan came bounding into it." He pronounced the great lion's name with an "s" rather than a "z" sound.[4]

These books are full of sights and sounds that Lewis knew. Children lived outside of London to avoid air raids. Kirkpatrick inspired both Professor Kirke's name and his grumbling about schools. The wardrobe in the story was from Little Lea. Lewis owned one that had been carved by his grandfather. A Lewis cousin identified the wardrobe now at the Wade Center in Wheaton, Illinois, as the one where the cousins sat while Jack Lewis told them stories.[5]

Many elements come from his reading. He used incidents from Greek and Roman authors. He drew from King Arthur, *Beowulf*, and English authors Geoffrey Chaucer, William Shakespeare, and John Milton. Lewis specifically names *The Arabian Nights*, *Alice's Adventures in Wonderland*, *Huckleberry Finn*, *Treasure Island*, Sherlock Holmes, and stories by E. Nesbit.[6] He put in dwarves, fauns, and talking animals. He even included Father Christmas.

Tolkien was shocked by the hodgepodge and particularly objected to a faun being portrayed as a friendly, social being, unlike those in mythology. He remarked to Green, "I hear you've been reading Jack's children's story. It really won't do, you know!"[7]

With no plan for additional titles, the events in the stories are not in sequence with publication. *The Horse and his Boy* (fifth) takes place near the end of the first book. Not until the sixth book, *The Magician's Nephew*, do readers learn that in his boyhood Professor Kirke planted the tree used to make the magic wardrobe.[8]

Narnia is a small country with an ocean on the east

that stretches beyond the sun to Aslan's home. To the north live the Marsh-wiggles and still farther north, the giants of Harfang. Narnia's sister country, Archenland, lies to the south. Farther south across a desert are the evil Calormenes. On the west, the Western Wild is full of mountains and dark forests. Lantern Waste, on the eastern edge of the Western Wild, is where Peter, Susan, Edmund, and Lucy first enter Narnia.[9]

In *The Lion, the Witch, and the Wardrobe*, the Pevensie children pass through the wardrobe into Narnia where the witch Jadis has made eternal winter. Jadis kills Aslan, but the lion comes back to life and restores peace.

The book is dedicated to Lewis's godchild Lucy Barfield. Even though Lewis worked quickly, he hints in his affectionate dedication that the book took a long time to write. In this case, the picture of the faun with the umbrella had been in his head since he was sixteen. Lewis often jotted down story ideas. Sometimes he found a note when he cleaned out a drawer and suddenly realized that he could finish the story.[10]

Prince Caspian, dedicated to Mary Clare Havard, opens with the four Pevensies being whisked back to Narnia when Prince Caspian blows Susan's old trumpet. The children restore Prince Caspian the Tenth to his throne with the help of the little mouse-knight Reepicheep and the walking trees. Gallant Reepicheep is one of Lewis's most loveable characters. Walking trees appear in ancient legends.

The Voyage of the "Dawn Treader" draws Lucy, Edmund, and obnoxious cousin Eustace into Narnia when the picture in Lucy's bedroom turns into a real ship. They encounter slave traders, storms, and sea serpents as they help King Caspian find his father's

A Lewis cousin identified this wardrobe as the one where C. S. Lewis often sat to tell the family his stories.

banished supporters. This book, dedicated to Geoffrey Barfield, is a contrast of emotions. Lewis provides humor in the book. He was a creature of habit who loved to eat. He has the Magician declare that all hungry times in his house are at one o'clock. On the dark side, Lewis suffered terrible nightmares much of his life. There is stark terror in the Dark Island where dreams come true.

The Silver Chair opens with Eustace helping his cousin Jill Pole escape from school bullies at Experiment House. With the help of Puddleglum the Marsh-wiggle, they rescue the mysterious knight tied to a silver chair by the Green Witch. In an earth-rending time, the chair is destroyed. The knight/prince returns to Narnia, and the bullies at Experiment House are punished.

The Silver Chair is dedicated to Nicholas Hardie, son of another Inkling Colin Hardie. Loveable Puddleglum is modeled on Paxford, the Kilns gardener who went around singing a funeral hymn.[11] In addition to making villains of school bullies, Lewis ridicules school administration by having the lunatic head of Experiment House lose her job for incompetence only to be given the position of inspecting other school heads.

In *The Horse and his Boy* a foundling named Shasta escapes a Calormene and flees on the talking horse, Bree. They are joined by Aravis racing on a beautiful talking mare named Hwin. Susan later joins their flight, as does Corin, who turns out to be Shasta's twin. This book is dedicated to David and Douglas Gresham, Joy's sons. The publisher rejected about ten titles before coming up with the eye-catching name himself.[12]

Lewis put his own preferences in this book. Shasta's real father quotes poetry. Evil Rabadash believes science improves everything. Lewis jabs at an educational system that does not let children exercise their imaginations. Instead of essays, he believed they should be encouraged to write stories. He makes the side comment, "I never heard of anyone who wanted to read the essays."[13]

The Magician's Nephew explains the origins of the lamppost and the wardrobe. Digory Kirke (the professor as a boy) and neighbor Polly Plummer are whisked into another world by magic rings. Witch Jadis follows them back. Aslan takes the iron bar Jadis rips off a London lamppost and turns it into the lamppost at Lantern Waste. Digory returns with the apple to cure his ill mother. The apple seeds are buried along with the magic rings. A tree springs up, and when it dies, Professor Kirke makes it into the wardrobe. Lewis spares Digory the sorrow of having his mother die. And, through Digory's voice, Lewis speaks his own belief, "I suppose all the old fairy tales are more or less true."[14]

Lewis dedicated *The Magician's Nephew* to the eight Kilmer children. They had begun writing to Lewis at the suggestion of their aunt, Mary Willis Shelburne, whose correspondence is found in *Letters to an American Lady*.[15]

The Last Battle pits the Calormenes and an evil ape named Shift in a final battle against good. The Calormenes win. The children, however, realize that they have died in a train wreck and gone to a place more beautiful than words can describe. Aslan tells them that they have left the earthly Shadow-Lands and have arrived in the true Narnia.

Lewis allows Emeth (Hebrew for "truth") to enter Narnia even though he had served the wrong master, simply because he sought truth. Lewis lightens the book's heavy subject with jokes—dogs call their puppies "boys" when they misbehave. Digory repeats the line, "What do they teach them at these schools!"[16]

In 1956 *The Last Battle* won the Carnegie Medal, British award for the best children's book. Forty years later, Philip Pullman won the same award. He strongly reacted against Lewis's book. He felt that a book where all the main characters die was not fit for children.[17]

Other readers are not disturbed by this. They consider *The Last Battle* a religious statement. They liken Aslan to Jesus and Narnia to heaven. They feel Aslan's urging the children to go deeper into Narnia is a way of saying that death is not the end but only the beginning of something better. Lewis often expressed this idea.[18]

CHAPTER 14

"I Sleep But My Heart Watcheth"

It is not hard to see why people who knew Lewis called him "the best–read man of his generation, one who read everything and remembered everything he read." A former student wrote Lewis asking for the source of a Latin inscription on a relative's tombstone. Lewis responded that it was from Song of Solomon 5:2. He translated it, "I am sleeping. But my heart is awake."[1]

Lewis not only read books but re-read them. A few weeks before his death, he was again reading his beloved *Iliad*. "[O]ther men simply read . . . [and] think that settles the matter. It is as if a man said he had once washed, or once slept, or once kissed his wife."[2]

His reading turned into scholarly books that ordinary people could read and books for ordinary people that brought extraordinary results. He may have described himself as a dinosaur because he enjoyed ancient writings, but nobody questioned his ability to set down arresting ideas for a modern reader.

To close friends, he was an interesting companion. George Sayers found him "highly persuasive, quite comical and very entertaining. Above all, he loved a good argument and he rarely passed up a chance to jump into the thick of things." Griffiths thought Lewis had "the most exact and penetrating mind" that he had ever encountered. Barfield, a sharp thinker, felt slow-witted in Lewis's company.[3]

Lewis had a puckish sense of humor. The Society for the Prevention of Progress, a California group, offered him membership. He replied that he would try to win their approval by "unremitting practice of Reaction, Obstruction, and Stagnation."[4]

His creative mind saw stories everywhere. Once while walking, Lewis was surrounded by pigs. Lewis scratched one with his cane and announced that this was no ordinary pig. It was a pog. *The Pig and the Pog.* That's not a bad title. Wonder if I can write the story to go with it. I must think about it."[5]

He knew five languages, but he spoke the language of children. He could correspond with a child about her hamster. He swung on swings with the Harwood children. He drew pictures with them. When they went swimming, he would come up from a dive and launch into a long philosophical discourse that sent them into shrieks of laughter.[6]

Universities honored him. St. Andrews in Scotland gave him an honorary Doctor of Divinity in 1946. Laval University, Quebec, Canada, awarded him an honorary Doctorate of Literature in 1952. He was a Fellow of the British Academy. But he turned down the highest British civilian honor, the Cross of the British Empire.[7]

He was completely unmoved by his fame. His driver during his Cambridge days remarked, "His learning may have been formidable but not the man himself." A friend sent him beautifully bound copies of *Surprised by Joy* and *Mere Christianity*. Perhaps, he mused, they would convince him to value his own works as he did those of other authors. Somehow, compared to "scratchy, inky" manuscripts, they did not seem real.[8]

Lewis's books and ideas continue to have an impact. More than fifty years after its publication, *Mere Christianity* caused Thomas S. Monaghan, the founder of Domino's Pizza, to abandon construction on a $7 million mansion. He sold his luxury cars. In 1998, with money from the sale of Domino's, he set up a twenty-year program to give $900 million to Catholic charities and schools.[9]

Some twenty years after Lewis's death, BBC broadcast the film *Shadowlands*, based on his life with Joy Gresham. The movie was remade in 1993, starring Anthony Hopkins and Deborah Winger. In 2004 Armand Nicholi's *The Question of God: C. S. Lewis and Sigmund Freud Debate God, Love, Sex, and the Meaning of Life* aired on PBS. That same year *The Lion, the Witch, and the Wardrobe* was filmed in New Zealand. In 2005, the producer of the 1985 *Shadowlands* released a second film, *C. S. Lewis: The Man Who Created Narnia*.[10]

When he was forced to resign from Cambridge for health reasons, Lewis wrote to Green, "I am now unofficially an extinct volcano."[11]

Even so, extinct volcanoes have left a large mark on our landscape.

In His Own Words

The following quotations of C. S. Lewis were taken from a variety of sources published between 1958 and 1985.

On The Writing Process:

I have never actually "made a story." With me the process is much more like bird-watching. . . . I see pictures. Sometimes the pictures have a common flavor. . . . Keep quiet and watch and they will begin joining themselves."

> "C. S. Lewis"
> *Puffin Post*, IV:1, p. 17

[Y]ou must not believe all that authors tell you about how they wrote their books. This is not because they mean to tell lies. It is because a man writing a story is too excited about the story itself to sit back and notice how he is doing it . . . .

> "It All Began with a Picture . . ."
> *Of Other Worlds: Essays and Stories*, p. 42.

"The way for a person to develop a style is (a) to know exactly what he wants to say, and (b) to be sure he is saying exactly that."

> "Heaven, Earth, and Outer Space"
> in *Decision*, October 1963, p. 4.

"I've never started from a message or a moral . . . .
You find out what the moral is by writing the story."

> "Unreal Estates"
> *On Stories and Other Essays on Literature*,
> p. 145.

"They seem to fancy that a book trickles out of one
like a sigh or a tear."

> "On Criticism"
> *On Stories and Other Essays on Literature*,
> p. 135.

Every good writer knows that the more unusual the
scenes and events of his story are, the slighter, the
more ordinary, the more typical his persons should be.
Hence Gulliver is a commonplace little man and Alice
a commonplace little girl."

> "On Science Fiction"
> *Of Other Worlds: Essays and Stories*,
> pp. 64–65.

That's the worst of facts—they do cramp a fellow's
style.

> *Letters of C. S. Lewis*, p. 127.

About his books:

"I don't want my dog to bark approval of my books.
Now that I come to think of it, there are some humans
whose enthusiastically favorable criticism would not
much gratify me."

> *Reflections on the Psalms*, p. 93.

"Some of the allegories thus imposed on my own
books have been so ingenious and interesting that I
often wish I had thought of them myself."

> *Reflections on the Psalms*, p. 100.

"[I]f you are often reviewed you will find yourself repeatedly blamed and praised for saying what you never said and for not saying what you have said."

> "On Criticism"
> *On Stories and Other Essays on Literature*,
> pp. 130–131.

Reading Choices:

"No book is really worth reading at age ten which is not equally (and often far more) worth reading at the age of fifty—except, of course, books of information."

> "On Stories"
> *On Stories and Other Essays on Literature*,
> p. 14.

"A great myth is relevant as long as the predicament of humanity lasts."

> "The Mythopoeic Gift of Rider Haggard"
> *On Stories and Other Essays on Literature*,
> p. 100.

Sources used for this section:

Dorsett, Lyle W. and Marjorie Lamp Mead. *C. S. Lewis Letters to Children*. New York: Simon & Schuster/Touchstone, 1985.

Green, Roger Lancelyn. "C. S. Lewis." *Puffin Post*, IV:1.

Lewis, C. S. *Letters of C. S. Lewis*. Edited by W. H. Lewis. New York: Harcourt, Brace & World, 1966.

Lewis, C. S. *Of Other Worlds; Essays and Stories*. New York: Harcourt, Brace & World, Inc., 1966.

Lewis, C. S. *On Stories and Other Essays on Literature*. Edited by Walter Hooper. New York: Harcourt Brace Jovanovich, Publishers, 1982.

Lewis, C. S. *Reflections on the Psalms*. London: Geoffrey Bles, 1958.

Timeline

1898— Born November 29 in Belfast, (Northern) Ireland.

1905— Moves to Little Lea.

1908— Flora Lewis dies; enrolls at Wynyard School.

1911— Transfers to Cherbourg School; loses faith in God.

1913— Enters Malvern College.

1914— Meets Arthur Greeves; begins study with Kirkpatrick.

1916— Takes Oxford exams.

1917— Enters University College, Oxford; called into military service; meets Janie Moore; is shipped to France.

1918— Wounded by British shell.

1919— Returns to Oxford; *Spirits of Bondage*, published.

1920— Receives a First in Honor Moderations (Greek and Latin Literature).

1922— Receives a First in Greats (Philosophy and Ancient History).

1923— Receives a First in English.

1924— Tutors philosophy while a professor on sabbatical.

1925— Elected fellow of Magdalen College, Oxford; tutored English Language and Literature.

1926— *Dymer* is published under pseudonym Clive Hamilton.

1929— Returns to belief in God; Albert Lewis dies.

1930— Purchases the Kilns with brother and Mrs. Moore.

1931— Becomes a Christian through Tolkien and Dyson.

1932— Warren Lewis retires, lives with brother.

1933— *The Pilgrim's Regress* published.

1936— *The Allegory of Love* published.

1938— *Out of the Silent Planet* published.

1940— *The Problem of Pain* published.

1941— *The Screwtape Letters* published.

1941–1944—Series of broadcasts for BBC radio; talks to military servicemen; sermons.

1943— *The Abolition of Man* and *Perelandra* published.

1945— *That Hideous Strength* and *The Great Divorce* published.

1946— Receives honorary Doctor of Divinity from University of St. Andrews, Scotland.

1947— *Miracles* published.

1950— *The Lion, the Witch, and the Wardrobe* published.

1951— *Prince Caspian* published; Janie Moore dies.

1952— Meets Joy Davidman Gresham; receives honorary Doctor of Literature from Laval University, Quebec, Canada; *Mere Christianity* and *Voyage of the Dawn Treader* are published.

1953— *The Silver Chair* published.

1954— *English Literature in the Sixteenth Century, Excluding Drama* (Oxford History of English Literature series) and *The Horse and his Boy* published.

1955— Moves to Cambridge University as Chair of Medieval and Renaissance Literature; *The Magician's Nephew* and *Surprised by Joy* published.

1956— April 23: Marries Joy Davidman Gresham in civil ceremony; *The Last Battle* and *Till We Have Faces* published.

1957— March 21: Religious marriage ceremony takes place at hospital.

1958— Elected honorary Fellow of University College, Oxford; *Reflections on the Psalms* published.

1960— July 13: Joy dies; *The Four Loves* and *Studies in Words* published.

1961— *A Grief Observed* published as N. W. Clerk.

1963— Resigns position at Cambridge; elected honorary Fellow of Magdalene College, Cambridge; dies November 22 and is buried at Holy Trinity Church, Headington Quarry, Oxford.

Chapter Notes

Chapter 1. The Little End Room

1. C. S. Lewis, *The Voyage of the Dawn Treader* (New York: Collier Books, 1952) p. 1.
2. *Letters of C. S. Lewis*, ed. W. H. Lewis (New York: Harcourt, Brace & World, Inc., 1966), p. 2.
3. Ibid. p. 1.
4. C. S. Lewis, *Surprised by Joy: The Shape of my Early Life* (New York: Harcourt Brace and Company, 1955), p. 123.
5. *Lewis Papers: Memoirs of the Lewis Family 1850–1930*, ed. Warren Hamilton Lewis (Bound typescript. Leeborough Press, 1933), vol. I, p. 326.
6. *Surprised*, p. 42.
7. *Lewis Papers*, vol. I, p. 329.
8. C. S. Lewis, *Collected Letters, Volume 1: Family Letters 1905–1931*, Walter Hooper, ed. (London: HarperCollins Publishers, 2000), p. 1009; *Lewis Papers*, vol.II, pp. 278–279.
9. *Lewis Papers*, vol. II, p. 314; *Letters*, p. 2.
10. Lyle W. Dorsett and Marjorie Lamp Mead, eds., *C. S. Lewis, Letters to Children* (New York: Simon & Schuster, 1985), pp. 37, 46.
11. *Lewis Papers*, vol .II, pp. 306, 322; Clyde S. Kilby, in Carolyn Keefe, ed., *C. S. Lewis, Speaker & Teacher* (Grand Rapids, MI: Zondervan Publishing House, 1971), p. 20.

12. *Surprised*, pp. 40, 43; *Collected Letters, Volume 1*, p. 461.
13. *Surprised*, p. 11.
14. Ibid., pp. 11, 154.
15. *Letters*, p. 2.
16. *Collected Letters, Volume 1*, p. 864; *Surprised*, pp. 14–15.
17. Walter Hooper, ed., *Boxen: The Imaginary World of the Young C. S. Lewis* (San Diego: Harcourt Brace Jovanovich, 1985), pp. 8, 58.
18. *Collected Letters, Volume 1*, p. 997; *Lewis Papers*, vol.II, pp. 297–299.
19. *Boxen*, p. 10.
20. Ibid., p. 206.
21. *Surprised*, p. 12; *Letters to Children*, p. 95.
22. *Surprised*, pp. 2–4, 11.
23. Ibid., p. 48.
24. Ibid., pp. 8–9, 46.
25. C. S. Lewis, "On Three Ways of Writing for Children," *The Horn Book Magazine*, October, 1963, p. 464.
26. *Surprised*, pp. 16, 5.
27. Ibid., pp. 7, 16–17.
28. *Lewis Papers*, vol. III, p. 120; Douglas Gilbert and Clyde S. Kilby, *C. S. Lewis: Images of His World* (Grand Rapids, Michigan: William B. Eerdmans Publishing Company, 1983), p. 183.
29. *Surprised*, pp. 21, 19.
30. Ibid., p. 23.

Chapter 2. "Are Athletes Better than Scholars?"
1. *Surprised*, p. 24
2. Ibid, pp. 25, 34; *Lewis Papers*. vol.III, p. 40.
3. *Lewis Papers*, vol.III, p. 147.

4. *Collected Letters, Volume 1*, p. 9.
5. *Surprised*, pp. 34, 130.
6. *Collected Letters, Volume 1*, pp. 12–13.
7. A.N. Wilson, *C. S. Lewis, a Biography* (London: Collins, 1990), p. 23.
8. *Collected Letters, Volume 1*, p. 15; *Surprised*, p. 25.
9. *Surprised*, pp. 44–45.
10. Roger Lancelyn Green and Walter Hooper, *C. S. Lewis; a Biography* (New York: Harcourt Brace and Jovanovich, 1974), p. 28; *Collected Letters*, Volume I, p. 96; *Surprised*, pp. 46–47.
11. *Surprised*, p. 53; *Letters to Children*, p. 46.
12. *Surprised*, pp. 54–55; *Letters*, pp. 159–160.
13. Wilson, pp. 27, 28.
14. *Letters*, p. 267.
15. *Surprised*, p. 57.
16. Ibid., pp. 16–17; 73.
17. James T. Como, ed. *C. S. Lewis at the Breakfast table and Other Reminiscences* (San Diego: Harcourt Brace & Company, 1992), p. 257.
18. *Letters*, p. 4; Wilson, p. 31.
19. *Lewis Papers*, vol. IV, p. 184.
20. *Surprised*, pp. 113–114.
21. *Letters*, p. 4; *Lewis Papers*, vol. X, pp. 142–143.
22. *Surprised*, pp. 110–114; Wilson, p. 34–35.
23. *Surprised*, pp. 73–76; 115.
24. Ibid. p. 78.
25. Ibid., p. 130.
26. *Letters*, p. 31.
27. *Surprised*, p. 158.

Chapter 3. "Never, Never, Never Shall I Have to Play Games Again"

1. Wilson, pp. 38–39.
2. *Surprised*, p. 129.
3. Ibid., p. 132.
4. *Lewis Papers*, vol. IV, p. 223.
5. *Surprised*, p. 148.
6. Ibid. pp. 133–136.
7. Green and Hooper, p. 41; *Letters to Children*, p. 44.
8. *Surprised*, pp. 140–141.
9. Ibid., pp. 144–145.
10. Ibid., p. 142.
11. Ibid., pp. 146,156.
12. Ibid., pp. 143, 147, 165; *Letters*, p. 33.
13. *Lewis Papers*, vol. IV, p. 250; *Collected Letters*, p. 258.
14. *Surprised*, pp. 151, 164, 203, 214.; C. S. Lewis, "Unreal Estates," in *On Stories and Other Essays on Literature*, Walter Hooper, ed. (New York: Harcourt Brace Jovanovich, Publishers, 1982), p. 146.
15. *Letters*, p. 27.
16. C. S. Lewis, *They Stand Together: The Letters of C. S. Lewis to Arthur Greeves (1914–1963)* Walter Hooper, ed. (New York: Macmillan Publishing Co., Inc., 1979), p. 135.
17. *Surprised*, pp. 179, 181.
18. Ibid., p. 183.
19. Ibid., p. 184.
20. Ibid., p. 186.

Chapter 4. "Death in Battle"

1. *Letters*, p. 34.
2. Ibid., pp. 8, 34.
3. Ibid., pp. 37, 40.
4. Ibid., p. 8; Wilson, p. 53.
5. Lady Dunbar (Maureen Moore Blake) in Wilson, p. 56.
6. *Surprised*, p. 188.
7. *Surprised*, pp. 189, 195; *Letters*, pp. 41, 45.
8. *Surprised*, p. 189.
9. Ibid., p. 197; *Collected Letters, Volume 1*, p. 366.
10. *Collected Letters, Volume 1*, pp. 367; Green and Hooper, p. 177.
11. *Collected Letters* Volume 1, pp. 385.
12. *Letters*, pp. 42–44.
13. *Lewis Papers*, vol.VI, pp. 44–45.
14. *Surprised*, pp. 191–193, 196.
15. *Letters*, p. 9.
16. Ibid., pp. 45–46.
17. *Collected Letters, Volume 1*, p. 399.
18. *Lewis Papers*, vol.VI, p. 104; *Letters*, p. 48.

Chapter 5. "I Love Every Stone of It"

1. *Letters*, p. 33; Lewis, quoted in Green and Hooper, p. 52.
2. *Surprised*, p. 187.
3. James Houston, in David Graham, ed. *We Remember C. S. Lewis: Essays & Memoirs* (Nashville, Tennessee: Broadman & Holman Publishers, 2001), p. 140.
4. *They Stand*, p. 242.
5. *Letters*, p. 12.
6. Ibid., p. 48.

7. Hooper, in Keefe, p. 39; *Letters*, p. 48.

8. *Letters*, pp. 11, 50

9. *Collected Letters*, p. 562.

10. *Letters*, p. 54.

11. *Surprised*, p. 74.

12. Ibid., p. 212.

13. *Collected Letters*, pp. 600, 611.

14. *Lewis Papers*, vol.VIII, pp. 225–226.

15. *Letters*, pp. 97, 99.

16. *Letters*, pp. 101–102.

17. *Lewis Papers*, vol.VIII, p. 290.

Chapter 6. "Too Much Straw and Not Enough Bricks"

1. *Letters*, p. 104.

2. Humphrey Carpenter, *The Inklings: C. S. Lewis, J. R. R. Tolkien, Charles Williams, and Their Friends* (Boston: Houghton Mifflin, 1979), pp. 128–129; Graham, p. 80.

3. *Letters*, pp. 104, 225.

4. Ibid., p. 15.

5. Patricia M. Hunt, in Graham, p. 57; W. J. B. Owen, in Graham, p. 59; Rosamund Cowen, in Stephen Schofield, ed., *In Search of C. S. Lewis* (South Plainfield, NJ: Bridge Publishing, Inc., 1983), p. 62.

6. George Bailey, in Keefe, p. 81; Derek Brewer, in Como, p. 62.

7. Brewer, in Como, p. 47.

8. Bailey, in Keefe, p. 87.

9. O'Hare, in Graham, p. 43.

10. Carpenter, p. 26.

11. *Letters*, p. 107; Cowan, in Schofield, p. 62; Penelope Fitzgerald, in Graham, p. 153.

12. Bailey, in Keefe, p. 83; H. M. Blamires, as quoted in *Letters*, p. 18.
13. Carpenter, p. 129.
14. *Collected Letters, Volume 1*, p. 749.
15. *Letters*, p. 123.
16. *Collected Letters, Volume 1*, p. 749.
17. Hugh Sinclair, in Graham, p. 116.
18. Green and Hooper, pp. 123–124.

Chapter 7. "As Good as an Extra Maid"

1. Jill Freud, in Schofield, p. 58; *Letters*, p. 195.
2. *Collected Letters, Volume 1*, p. 1020; Fred W. Paxford, in Graham, p. 123; *Letters*, p. 16.
3. Green and Hooper, p. 123.
4. *Lewis Papers*, vol.VI, pp. 141–142; *Letters*, p. 21.
5. *Surprised*, p. 215.
6. *Collected Letters, Volume 1*, p. 827.
7. Ibid., pp. 842–844.
8. Ibid., p. 864; *Lewis Papers*, vol.X, p. 207, vol.XI, p. 5.
9. "St. Mark's and C S Lewis" n.d., <http://ireland.iol.ie/~coiace/lewis.html> (January 2, 2005).
10. Carpenter, p. 38; *Collected Letters, Volume 1*, p. 265.
11. *Letters*, p. 172.
12. Carpenter, p. 130.
13. *Letters*, p. 94; *They Stand*, pp. 513, 566.
14. Warren Lewis, as quoted in Carpenter, pp. 38–39.
15. Paxford, in Graham, pp. 120–124.
16. C. S. Lewis, *Letters to an American Lady*, Clyde Kilby, ed., (Grand Rapids, Michigan: William B. Eerdmans Publishing Company, 1967), p. 45; Carpenter, p. 207; Brewer, in Como, p. 60.

17. *Collected Letters, Volume 1*, p. 1013.
18. Justin Phillips, *C. S. Lewis at the BBC: Messages of Hope in the Darkness of War* (London: HarperCollins Publishers, 2002), pp. 81, 86; Brewer, in Como, p. 45.
19. Carpenter, p. 53.
20. *Letters*, p. 22; Patricia Heidelberger, in Schofield, p. 53–54.
21. Freud, in Schofield, pp. 56–57.
22. Wilson, p. 187; Freud, in Schofield, p. 56.
23. Lewis, as quoted in Wilson, p. 203.
24. Freud, in Schofield, 57; Heidelberger, in Schofield, p. 54.
25. Armand M. Nicholi, Jr., *The Question of God: C. S. Lewis and Sigmund Freud Debate God, Love, Sex, and the meaning of Life* (New York: The Free Press, 2002), p. 4.
26. *Letters*, pp. 195, 212.
27. *Collected Letters, Volume 1*, p. 987.
28. *Letters*, p. 232.

Chapter 8. "Has Nobody Got Anything to Read Us?"

1. "Tolkien, J.R.R.," in Colin Duriez, *The C. S. Lewis Encyclopedia* (Wheaton, Illinois: Crossway Books, 2000), pp. 208–209; *Collected Letters, Volume 1*, p. 1023.
2. *They Stand*, p .341; *Lewis Papers*, vol. IX, pp. 156–157.
3. *They Stand*, p. 449; Carpenter, pp. 30, 65, 32.
4. Carpenter, p. 227; "Tolkien's *The Lord of the Rings*," in *On Stories*, p. 83.
5. Carpenter, p. 122.
6. Ibid., p. 67.
7. *Letters*, 16, 115; *Lewis Papers*, vol. IX, p. 229.

8. Carpenter, pp. 209–210.
9. *Letters*, pp. 13, 287.
10. Carpenter, p. 176; *Collected Letters*, p. 1013.
11. Carpenter, pp. 176–178; *Letters*, p. 14.
12. Green and Hooper, p. 75; Wilson, pp. 80, 105; *Collected Letters, Volume 1*, pp. 984–986.
13. *Surprised*, pp. 199–200, 204; "Barfield, Owen" in *Collected Letters, Volume 2: Books, Broadcast and War, 1931–1945*, p. 1017.
14. *Collected Letters, Volume 1*, pp. 997–1000.
16. *The Letters of J. R. R. Tolkien*, ed. by Humphrey Carpenter (Boston: Houghton Mifflin, 1981), p. 130.
17. Carpenter, p. 116; *Letters*, p. 170.
18. Carpenter, p. 119; *Letters*, p. 206; Carpenter, p. 121.
19. Carpenter, p. 226.

Chapter 9. "I Never Thought to Have . . ."

1. *Letters*, p. 55.
2. Carpenter, p. 234; Chad Walsh, "Afterword," in C. S. Lewis, *A Grief Observed* (New York: Bantam Books, 1962), p. 137.
3. *Grief Observed*, p. 138; Carpenter, p. 236.
4. Carpenter, p. 236.
5. *Grief Observed*, p. 3.
6. Carpenter, p. 237.
7. Green and Hooper, 259.
8. Wilson, p. 246.
9. *Letters to an American Lady*, p. 33.
10. Green and Hooper, pp. 284–285.
11. Carpenter, p. 231.
12. Walsh, in *Grief Observed*, p. 140.
13. Green and Hooper, p. 268.

14. Carpenter, p. 241; Peter Bayley, in Como, p. 86.
15. *Letters*, pp. 22–23.
16. Ibid., p. 280.
17. Green and Hooper, p. 270.
18. Carpenter, p. 248.
19. *Grief Observed*, pp. 1, 2.
20. Green and Hooper, p. 277.
21. *Collected Letters*, p. 987.
22. *Letters*, p. 307; *They Stand*, p. 566.
23. Richard Ladborough, in Como, p. 104; Green and Hooper, p. 306.
24. Bayley, in Como, p. 86; Wilson, p. 299.
25. *Letters of J. R. R. Tolkien*, p. 341.
26. Douglas and Kilby, pp. 182–183.

Chapter 10. "It Is Always Better to Read Chaucer Again . . ."

1. *Letters*, p. 260.
2. *Letters of J. R. R. Tolkien*, p. 388; C. S. Lewis and Don Giovanni Calabria, *The Latin Letters of C. S. Lewis* (South Bend, Indiana: St. Augustine's Press, 1998), pp. 105–106; Carpenter, pp. 47–48.
3. *Letters*, pp. 73,76.
4. *Letters*, p. 127.
5. Green and Hooper, p. 160; Joe Christopher, *C. S. Lewis* (Boston: Twayne Publishers, 1987), pp. 23, 26.
6. Wilson, p. 145; Chad Walsh, *The Literary Legacy of C. S. Lewis* (New York: Harcourt, Brace, Jovanovich, 1979), p. 195; Christopher, p. 24.
7. Wilson, p. 147.
8. Christopher, p. 42.
9. Carpenter, p. 224.
10. Helen Gardner, in Duriez, p. 174; *Letters*, p. 10.
11. Wilson, p. 241; Christopher, p. 27.

12. Christopher, pp. 34–35.
13. Lewis, as quoted in Wilson, p. 289.
14. Brewer, in Como, p. 47; Kenneth Tynan, in Schofield, pp. 6–7.
15. Christopher, p. 33.

Chapter 11. "Pseudo-Bunyan's Periplus"

1. *Surprised*, pp. 11, 139, 174.
2. *Letters*, pp. 56–57; *Surprised*, p. 213.
3. *Surprised*, pp. 223–224.
4. *Collected Letters, Volume 1*, pp. 969–970.
5. *Letters*, pp. 19, 154.
6. Carpenter, pp. 51–52.
7. Wilson, p. 174.
8. *Surprised*, p. 172; *Letters*, p. 100.
9. Martin Moynihan, in Graham, p. 39.
10. Green and Hooper, pp. 128–130.
11. J. I. Packer, in Graham, p. 30; *Letters*, pp. 248–249.
12. Clyde Kilby, *The Christian World of C. S. Lewis* (Grand Rapids, Michigan: Wm. B. Eerdmans Publishing Company, 1964), p. 31; *Letters*, p. 180.
13. C. S. Lewis, *The Problem of Pain* (New York: The Macmillan Company, 1962), p. 93; George Sayer, in Como, p. 202.
14. Stuart Barton Babbage, in Keefe, pp. 72–73; Kilby, in Keefe, p. 19.
15. Phillips, p. 114.
16. Como, p. 252.
17. Cooke, as quoted in Keefe, p. 117.
18. Charles Colson, in Graham, pp. 26–27.
19. *Letters*, p. 188; Lewis, as quoted in Carpenter, p. 176.

20. Helen Tyrell Wheeler, in Graham, p. 50; Carpenter, p. 176.
21. Green and Hooper, p. 198,199; "Don v. Devil," *Time*, September 8, 1947, pp. 65–66.
22. Tolkien, as quoted in Carpenter, p. 194.
23. Joe Christopher, *C. S. Lewis* (Boston: Twayne Publishers, 1987), p. 73.
24. Keefe, pp. 122, 125.
25. Kilby, *Christian World*, p. 73–77; *Letters*, p. 256.
26. Green and Hooper, p. 198; *Collected Letters, Volume 1*, p. 981.
27. Christopher, pp. 83–85.

Chapter 12. "Nothing in Nature Is *Quite* Regular"

1. *Letters of J. R. R. Tolkien*, pp. 209, 342; Carpenter, pp. 65–66.
2. *Letters of J. R. R. Tolkien*, p. 224; *Letters*, pp. 244–245, 284.
3. Paxford, in Graham, p. 126.
4. *Letters*, p. 205; "A Reply to Professor Haldane," in *On Stories*, p. 71; C. S. Lewis, *That Hideous Strength: A Modern Fairy Tale for Grown-ups* (New York: Macmillan Publishing Co., Inc., 1946) p. 268.
5. S. E. Wirt, "Heaven, Earth and Outer Space," *Decision*, October 1963, p. 4.
6. *Letters*, p. 166.
7. Carpenter, p. 182.
8. Ibid., p. 193.
9. *Letters*, p. 283.
10. C. S. Lewis, "Vivisection," London: The National Anti-Vivisection Society, written for the New England Anti-Vivisection Society, undated.
11. Christopher, p. 102; Green and Hooper, p. 265.

Chapter 13. "Aslan Came Bounding Into It"

1. "On Three Ways of Writing for Children," p. 464.
2. Dorsett and Mead, p. 31; Green and Hooper, pp. 244–247.
3. Green and Hooper, pp. 243, 246.
4. "It All Began With a Picture . . . ;" in C. S. Lewis, *Of Other Worlds: Essays and Stories*, Walter Hooper, ed. (New York: Harcourt, Brace & World, 1966), p. 42; Dorsett and Mead, p. 29.
5. Author interview with Marjorie Lamp Mead, Wheaton, Illinois, July 22, 2004.
6. M. A. Manzalaoui, in Graham, p. 16
7. Tolkien, as quoted in Green and Hooper, p. 241.
8. Kilby, *Christian World*, p. 131.
9. Kilby, *Christian World*, pp. 121–122.
10. "It All Began with a Picture . . . ", p. 42; Dorsett and Mead, p. 95.
11. Green and Hooper, p. 254.
12. Green and Hooper, p. 245.
13. C. S. Lewis, *The Horse and his Boy* (New York: Collier Books, 1954), p. 32.
14. C. S. Lewis, *The Magician's Nephew* (New York: Collier Books, 1955), p. 24.
15. Dorsett and Mead, pp. 38, 40.
16. C. S. Lewis, *The Last Battle* (New York: Collier Books, 1956), p. 170.
17. Pullman, in Phillips, p. 292
18. Marjorie E. Wright, in Kilby, *Christian World*, p. 200.

Chapter 14. "I Sleep But My Heart Watcheth"

1. William Empson, in Duriez, p. 174; Moynihan, in Graham, p. 40.

2. Green and Hooper, p. 206; "Different Tastes in Literature," *On Stories*, p. 120.

3. George Sayer, as quoted in Phillips, p. 106; Griffiths, as quoted in Kilby, *Christian World*, p. 12; Barfield, in Keefe, p. 104.

4. *Letters*, p. 204.

5. Sayer, in Como, p. 209

6. A. C. Harwood, in Como, p. 238.

7. Green and Hooper, p. 306; *Letters*, p. 235.

8. Clifford Morris, in Como, p. 197; *Letters*, p. 259.

9. Domenica Marchetti, "Delivering on His Word: Pizza-empire funder is giving away his fortune to Catholic causes," *The Chronicle of Philanthropy; Gifts & Grants*, October 7, 1999 <http://philanthropy.com/free/articles/v11/i24/24000101.htm> (June 28, 2004).

10. Graham, p,79; Barbara Karkabi, "Opposite convictions, parallel lives," *Houston Chronicle*, September 11, 2004; "Filming Has Wrapped," <http://www.narniaweb.com/news.asp?id=159> (January 2, 2005); Senay Boztas, "Movie makers give C. S. Lewis Lord Of the Rings treatment" <http://www.sundayherald.com45577> (February 14, 2005).

11. Lewis, as quoted in Green and Hooper, p. 303.

Glossary

articulated—To be put into spoken words.

atheist—Someone who does not believe in God.

cataract—Large waterfall or turbulent water.

chalice—Cup or goblet.

chancellor—High officer or president of a university.

charitable trust—A fund of money set aside for charity purposes.

discourse—A lengthy talk on a subject.

expeditionary—Engaged in a military operation.

faun—Imaginary creature with a man's body and legs of a goat.

folio—A large manuscript of folded sheets.

hippodrome—An arena or theater.

inconsolable—Not able to be consoled or comforted.

literary—Related to literature and books.

megaphone—A funnel-shaped horn that makes a speaker's voice louder.

natural law—The rules of nature.

optimism—Believing that the best will happen. In philosophy, the belief that good triumphs over evil.

philologist—One who studies the history of words.

plagiarism—Claiming as one's own something written by someone else.

popular—Well-liked. In literature, works the general public reads.

prolegomena—An introduction.

pseudo—A prefix meaning "false."

recuperation—A time of recovery from illness.

Renaissance—Revival of learning and the arts.

scathing—Extremely harsh.

shrouded—Covered, wrapped in cloth.

Socratic—Related to Socrates and his use of debate to learn truth.

spats—A cloth covering the upper shoe.

stagnation—Stale, lifeless, failing to move.

tankard—A large drinking cup with a handle and sometimes a hinged lid.

trilogy—A group of three books or plays.

unfettered—Without boundaries or restraints.

unorthodox—Not the traditional; unusual.

Valkyries—In Norse mythology, maidens who conducted the souls of slain heroes to Valhalla.

vaudeville—Slapstick stage entertainment.

viscount—A nobleman of lesser rank.

visa—Government document that allows foreigners to enter another country.

vocational training—Training for an occupation that does not require college study.

Selected Works of C. S. Lewis

Further Reading

Cording, Ruth James. *C. S. Lewis, A Celebration of his Early Life*. Nashville, TN: Broadman & Holman Publishers, 2000.

Coren, Michael. *The Man Who Created Narnia: The Story of C. S. Lewis*. Grand Rapids, MI: Wm. B. Eerdmans Publishing Co., 1994.

Gormley, Beatrice. *C. S. Lewis: Christian & Storyteller*. Grand Rapids, MI: Wm. B. Eerdmans Publishing Co., 1997.

Internet Addresses

C.S. Lewis Foundation
http://www.cslewis.org

C. S. Lewis: A Modest Literary Biography and Bibliography
http://personal.bgsu.edu/~edwards/biobib.html

Into the Wardrobe: a C. S. Lewis Web Site
http://cslewis.drzeus.net

Index